Praise for *Dating Radar*

"This highly readable, detailed guide is an indispensable manual to dating in the digital age. When technology has made it so simple to connect, but doesn't supply the wisdom or insight of a personal or community network, caution is more crucial now than ever. The authors offer clear, easy-to-follow advice and convincing stories from their wealth of expertise with high-conflict personalities. This is essential reading for anyone wanting to understand his or her blind spots when looking for love."

—ANNE MICHAUD,
author of *Why They Stay: Sex Scandals, Deals, and Hidden Agendas of Nine Political Wives*

"This book is great! As a person who helps people with high-conflict marriages, it does my heart good to have a book with the wisdom of authors like Bill Eddy and Megan Hunter, who try to prevent high-conflict marriages in the first place. People tell me 'I wish I had known about high-conflict partners 10-12 years ago.' To find out about them beforehand is a blessing, which may help people avoid years of hardship in an unhappy marriage with unhappy children. This gives binoculars for people to see beyond their childhood programming. Now they can look with fresh eyes before it's too late."

—RANDI KREGER,
author of *The Essential Family Guide to Borderline Personality Disorder* and co-author of *Stop Walking on Eggshells: Taking Your Life Back When Someone You Love Has Borderline*

D0950405

"Are you actually going to commit the rest of your life to that charming, good-looking person you found on an app? Are you blindly allowing momentum or neediness or loneliness or sex to push you into a future with a person you've known so briefly? Have you caught yourself rationalizing that 'he only hit me once' or 'she promised never to do that again' or 'I can change him?' Do you secretly worry that the exciting passion of the bedroom could easily turn into the corrosive passion of divorce? Then it's time to turn on and tune up your dating radar. Eddy and Hunter have given you the means. Now it's up to you to make healthy relationship choices."

—BENJAMIN D. GARBER, Ph.D.,

psychologist, author of *Holding Tight/Letting Go*, and *Developmental Psychology for Family Law Professionals*

"One of the most frustrating things for a divorce lawyer is the inability to help a client understand what went wrong in the relationship, so healing can start and the same mistakes aren't repeated. Megan Hunter and Bill Eddy's book explains, and goes far beyond dating advice: it's the equivalent of 20/20 foresight about relationships, delivered in a kind, frank, and intelligent way. This is the kind of book people bring to my office, crying with relief, saying 'This explains so much.'"

—ANNETTE BURNS,

Attorney and Mediator; President, Association of Family and Conciliation Courts (AFCC)

"Megan Hunter and Bill Eddy help readers navigate dating with a common sense approach and avoid the usual pitfalls that keep so many people single. It's an easy read that will surely provide transformative results in the reader's dating life."

—TAYLOR FRANÇOIS-BODINE,

Professional Matchmaker

Dating Radar

Why Your Brain Says Yes to
"The One"
Who Will Make Your Life Hell

Bill Eddy, LCSW, Esq.

Megan Hunter, MBA

UNHOOKED BOOKS
an imprint of High Conflict Institute Press
Scottsdale, Arizona

Copyright © 2017 by Bill Eddy and Megan Hunter
Unhooked Books, LLC
7701 E. Indian School Rd., Ste. F
Scottsdale, AZ 85251
www.unhookedbooks.com

ISBN: 978-1-936268-12-2
eISBN: 978-1-936268-13-9

Cover design by Julian Leon, The Missive
Interior layout by Jeffrey Fuller
Editor: Jess Beebe
Proofreader: Susan LaCroix

Website: www.dating-radar.com

Printed in the United States of America

A NOTE OF CAUTION
TO THE READER

This book provides information about avoiding relationships with people who may have high-conflict personalities. The information provided is intended to help you be more educated and aware of people who may cause relationship problems for you.

Knowledge is power. However, this high-conflict personality information can also be misused, which may inadvertently make your life more difficult. Therefore, we caution you not to publicly label high-conflict people in your life, not to tell people you think they have high-conflict personalities, nor to use this information as a weapon in personal relationships. Before you go further, we ask that you make a commitment to use this information with caution, compassion, and respect.

These explanations and information address general high-conflict behavior and may not apply to your specific situation. You are advised to seek the advice of a professional like a therapist, attorney, or law enforcement officer when warranted.

The authors and publisher are not responsible for any decisions or actions you take as a result of reading this book.

Please use caution in taking steps to terminate existing relationships if you suspect your partner may have a high-conflict personality.

Contents

*To Alice, who taught me that it IS possible to find
a wonderful life partner!*

—Bill Eddy

*To my beautiful mother-in-law, June, a survivor who gave me
the gift of Paul, the man who required no radar.*

—Megan Hunter

Dating Radar

Introduction

Radar was invented to detect danger that your eyes cannot see. What if you could develop radar to warn you of dating danger that your heart cannot see? We believe that you can.

But why would you need it? Maybe you've been in a highly toxic relationship before, and you'd like to avoid another one. Or you'd just like to be assured that you're not making a mistake before it's too late. Either way, this book will help. We all need dating radar to avoid a potentially miserable life.

Most people are still in the dark when it comes to picking the person they marry or commit to. If you're not already in a committed relationship, you're probably looking for one. And if you're in one, you may be basing your decision to fully commit to your partner based on an intense spark, charm, or sense of compatibility. You've fallen in love. Nothing wrong with that. But what if you found out that those same qualities that are genuinely a good sign in most relationships are the opposite in others? That they are actually potential red flags you should investigate further?

When it comes to love, the brain becomes irrational and shortsighted. We make decisions based on incomplete information, biased understanding, and strong emotions. Love truly is blind. That's why you need dating radar: it gives you a way to detect hazards you might otherwise miss. It gives you relationship intelligence.

So, are you looking for love? A life partner? Have you met someone who could turn out to be "the one"? Or maybe you've already found "the one" and just want to make sure you're not making a mistake before walking down the aisle or signing a lease on that condo.

Well, there's an important pitfall you'll want to watch out for. We're talking about "high-conflict people." They might look great on the surface, but sooner or later (usually within a year), they'll make your life a living hell with increasing conflicts, blame, chaos, and drama. While at first you may have been their target of seduction, you'll eventually turn into their *target of blame.* These folks are like reefs lurking just below the surface of the lovely tropical sea of love.

High-conflict people (HCPs) tend toward all-or-nothing thinking, unmanaged emotions, extreme behaviors or threats, and blaming others. But all of this may be well hidden from you at the start, because of their ability to jam your radar and because of your own dating blind spots (we all have them). Our goal is to help you in three ways, by showing you how to recognize:

1. Warning signs of certain personalities that can spell love relationship danger.
2. Ways that they can jam your radar (deceive you).
3. Where your own blind spots might be.

We focus on four high-conflict personality types, their common characteristics in romantic relationships, their common deceptions, and their targets' common blind spots. We give examples of how they deceive their targets and how their targets fool themselves—despite the warning signs. We want to help you steer clear of those reefs.

But why should you listen to us? Here's who we are:

Bill

For over thirty years, I have worked with children and families. First, I was a therapist for twelve years. Now I've been a family lawyer and divorce mediator for over twenty years. Altogether, I have helped approximately 2000 couples get divorced in and out of court. I have seen the pain of separating from a high-conflict partner hundreds of times.

I've counseled teenagers, some already in abusive dating relationships. I've helped couples get divorced, from their early twenties with children, to their mid-seventies with great-grandchildren. In some cases, they split up pretty quickly, and other times after decades of struggle. One woman said her twenty-seven-year marriage had been hell, and I asked for how long. "Twenty-six years," she said.

I represented a husband who was killed by his wife's new boyfriend in the middle of the divorce. In some cases, the divorce-from-hell lasted longer in family court than the marriage-from-hell. I've represented men and women about equally in family court, and worked with both together in divorce mediation—where sometimes one or the other will tell me it's been awful for years.

In most of these cases, they didn't see any warning signs in the beginning. Or they ignored them in hopes that things would get better. *Time and love,* they thought. Sometimes that's true, but not with high-conflict people. I want to help you avoid this experience. And it *is* avoidable. From working with my therapy and divorce clients, I have learned a lot about the warning signs, and I am glad to be able to share them with you in this book.

Personally, I have been happily married for thirty years. My wife, Alice, and I dated for a year, then lived together for about a year, then got married. Before we met, we each had some therapy to sort out prior relationship problems and figure out what we could each do differently. We didn't grow up knowing what we know now. Dating radar is something that has to be learned.

Megan

After graduating from college with a business degree and no idea what to do with my future, I started working in child support enforcement, and eventually I gravitated to family law—high-conflict cases in particular. Over the years, I've educated professionals on several continents; published books on relationships, conflict, abuse, and personality disorders; and written a book on complicated relationships. I am divorced, have been a single parent to three kids, and have been married eleven years to a kind, calm, wonderful man.

Before meeting my lovely husband, I dated a few men. Some were nice. Some weren't. Some were self-aware but also self-absorbed. Some were mean. Some just weren't that interesting. And then…there was the one with whom I had "the spark." He quickly charmed me, wooed me, and promised a life together, and I fell hook, line, and sinker for him and his promises. But just as quickly as I had fallen for him, he was gone and I was left broken-hearted and stupefied. What had happened? It was so perfect. He was my future! With the help of an excellent therapist, I set out to understand why I picked certain partners and how to do it differently in the future.

From my personal experiences combined with my work with high-conflict disputes, and training professionals in how to handle them, I've learned to quickly identify toxic or potentially toxic relationships. In fact, people think I must be psychic when I stop them early in their stories and fill in the blanks. But I'm not. High-conflict relationships are simply patterned and predictable.

I've taken countless calls from men who've just been released from jail, lost their jobs, aren't allowed to see their kids, all due to some type of violence allegations from a spouse or partner. I've been in a room at the Arizona State Capitol with fourteen women whose husbands had murdered their children, who were now trying to change child custody laws. I've listened to countless men and women recount their romance and divorce horror stories. I've observed impending relationship train wrecks from near and afar. And I've watched family members and friends step unwittingly into the minefield of a high-conflict relationship. From these experiences I've learned to predict what is likely to happen in relationships with high-conflict people.

This book is my opportunity to do what I like to do best—break barriers and challenge the status quo. I write from the perspective of a professional who has worked on the problem from many perspectives—legislative, training, consulting, coaching, and educating. I also write from my own perspective as someone who has experienced the minefield firsthand, and as a friend to many who've had similar experiences. Most importantly, I write as though I'm writing myself an instruction manual on what I wish I'd known about dating radar before I started dating, and what I want my kids to know as they choose their life partners. My hope is that your path to a happy relationship will be shorter than mine was, and that you will avoid the pain that a high-conflict partner would surely inflict.

Our Collaboration

The seeds of this book were planted when our lives intersected serendipitously in 2005.

In Megan's position as Family Law Specialist at the Arizona Supreme Court, Administrative Office of the Courts, she met with judges to hear their concerns and requests for training. The common thread among all of them was the trepidation they felt in cases in which accusations of domestic violence and child abuse—especially child sex abuse—were made against one of the parents. In some cases, they didn't know what to do because they didn't know how to tell who was telling the truth and who wasn't. They lost sleep over these cases. And typically, one—if not both—of the parents in the case blamed the judge for any bad outcome. They weren't bad judges; they just didn't have the background necessary to understand what was going on beneath the surface.

During the same time, Bill had begun writing articles and books about his experiences with high-conflict divorce and child custody cases. One of these articles appeared in a mediation newsletter that happened to land on Megan's desk. Bill's article switched on a lightbulb over Megan's head. It opened her eyes to understanding and managing the cases that were causing the judges so much trouble. It wasn't the particular situations and circumstances that drove these cases—it was what Bill called "high-conflict personalities."

Bill had uncovered the problem and discovered the solution. Using his background as a therapist helping people with personality disorders, he recognized those patterns of behavior in some of his divorce clients when he became a lawyer. Megan invited Bill to speak to Arizona's family court judges, and again a few months later to a group of child custody evaluators, whose projected attendance of thirty-five ballooned to nearly 200. After some respectful arm-twisting, Megan convinced Bill that everyone involved in divorce and child custody work needed this training.

Thus began our work together. In 2008, we cofounded the High Conflict Institute, as a resource for professionals and individuals dealing with high-conflict people. Through the Institute we work together on ideas, projects, and books, and over the years have trained tens of thousands of people around the globe in how to deal with high-conflict people in family court, in business and the workplace, and in life in general.

From numerous discussions about our work over the years, we decided that there was a great need for people to understand high-conflict personalities *before* they committed to their love relationships. We've heard far too many stories of people who thought they had found "the one," only to go through a traumatic breakup months, years, or even decades later. Many of these folks had kids, who ended up with scars lasting a lifetime. The adults, too, had scars, and in many cases the scars never healed. In fact, they often reopened as festering wounds that infected their other relationships.

We'd like to reverse the trend. We have important information to share—knowledge that can help you avoid relationship disaster. Unless you know someone who has been through a *War of the Roses* or *Fatal Attraction* relationship, or you've been through one yourself, you're probably naïve to the ins and outs of high-conflict people and the full extent of the damage they can cause—not just to their partner, but to nearly everyone around them. The shrapnel hits far and wide. These are relationships that range from extraordinarily exhausting and chaotic, to violent and even deadly.

It's serious. We wish we could sit down and have a heart-to-heart with everyone before they marry, move in with, or commit in some way to a person who is going to make their lives hell, but we can't. Instead, we've written this book to help you take steps to analyze your relationship risk by developing and fine-tuning your dating radar. We'd love to decrease the incidence of domestic violence, child abuse, and high-conflict divorce. We're committed to doing whatever we can to prevent all this bad stuff from happening to good people.

Our Survey

To help us include a broad range of information in this book, we developed an online survey for people to tell their stories and share their warning signs, deceptions, and blind spots. We received a few hundred responses. They generally confirmed our perceptions, but also gave us new insights into the lessons we want to share in this book. These responses are quoted throughout the book. (In some cases, we've made very minor edits, but the content and feel are true to the original in every case.) If you want to see the survey responses or want to share your own experiences, you can take the survey at **www.dating-radar.com.** Of course, this is not a scientific survey, but rather the opinions of those who heard about the survey. Still, people have shared a wide range of thoughts and experiences that have been helpful in fleshing out the information we offer in this book.

We both know that dating can be tricky and, at times, very painful. But we don't want you to give up. Instead, we want to help you improve your dating radar, so you can screen out high-conflict partners and find a truly satisfying relationship.

We hope that you find this book helpful, no matter what your age or where you are in the dating process. (You'll also find this book useful if you're trying to help one of your kids, a relative, friend, neighbor, client, parishioner...just about anyone.) We're glad you're looking for love—and we think the best way to find it is to keep your eyes open!

CHAPTER ONE

Who is a High-Conflict Person?
(and Why Should You Avoid Committing to One?)

Wouldn't it be helpful if people came with color-coded relationship-potential labels? Green for "All clear—go ahead." Yellow for "Caution—trouble ahead." Red for "Chaos, misery, and destruction—avoid at all costs." Think about it: if we (hopefully) reasonable folks picked people with green labels, our lives would be easier and less stressful, and our relationships would be more likely to succeed. The yellows and reds would be left to date each other, and we all know how *that* would go.

But people don't come with warning labels, and even if they did, we might not heed their colorful advice. The trouble with humans is that we often make decisions that are against our self-interest without realizing it, especially when love and lust are involved.

For better or for worse, it's up to us to pick good partners and make good decisions. Of course it's not a good idea to marry a serial killer, a stalker, or someone who treats us badly. Most of us manage to avoid these types. But if we're so good at screening partners, why does approximately half of the population end up divorced or in a relationship that doesn't last? And why do 10 to 20 percent of breakups escalate into all-out war? (If you're not sure what we mean by that, skip ahead a few pages to "Kelly's

Story".) We'd all like to know who will make our life complete and won't cause us misery, yet we are clearly not so good at telling the greens from the reds.

We don't have to drill down very far to discover that some of those divorces and break-ups are the result of destructive, chaotic, disastrous pairings that at one time felt happy and solid. Even when parents, friends, or others are able to identify impending relationship disaster, we ourselves can be blind to it. We look back after a disastrous relationship and wonder how we didn't see it. Where was our dating radar?

One of the most important decisions you'll make—who you'll share your life with—is often decided in a short time period without all of the information and without much thought to what could go wrong. Many of us have blinders on when it comes to love. We ignore advice from well-intentioned friends and family. We even disregard our own gut feelings, forging ahead to the altar. Others are more careful and proceed forward fully trusting that we've picked the right one but eventually get blind-sided.

How does it happen? Who is this person who makes our life hell? Probably someone with a *high-conflict personality*. And when a relationship has a high-conflict person in it, it becomes a high-conflict relationship.

High-conflict relationships are not just the worst; they're the worst of the worst. People with high-conflict personalities always find *targets of blame,* and attack them for causing all their problems. If you're in a relationship with a high-conflict person (HCP), you will eventually become their target. HCPs take no responsibility for their own behavior and their contribution to their own problems. They are toxic, chaotic, and exhausting. People who have been in relationships with high-conflict people describe the experience as one filled with dread, exhaustion, fear, and despair.

In every nasty divorce, or high-profile murder case like O.J. Simpson and Nicole Brown Simpson or Jodi Arias and her boyfriend, Travis Alexander, it's likely that at least one of them has a high-conflict personality. Nearly every movie and television show that depicts an antagonistic couple suggests one or two high-conflict partners. In fact, television and movies would be boring or nonexistent without this explosive kind of romance.

But some troubled partnerships are hard to spot. The majority of the most difficult "difficult" relationships are more nuanced than the ones you see on screen. The toxicity may not be as obvious, but the couple is still in store for major distress and at high risk of divorce, violence, or even lifelong depression or substance abuse. People in relationships with HCPs are living in misery. They may go outside the relationship to find relief, love, compassion—anything to make life more bearable.

Clearly, it's worthwhile to avoid high-conflict partners. To do this, you'll need to be able to recognize even the more subtle ones. By the end of this book, you will know how to identify who should get the green light, when you should proceed with caution, and when you should change your number and block on social media. In this chapter, we'll take a closer look at high-conflict people and the relationship havoc they wreak.

Our Dilemma in Writing This Book

Before going further, let's talk about the inherent conflict that comes from placing a warning sign on a group of people—those you shouldn't marry or commit to. We, as authors and experts in this area, struggle with this conflict. Both of us are "helping" professionals—natural givers of empathy and compassion—so having this knowledge puts us in a tough spot. The very people we are warning you to avoid romantically are the same people who need help the most. However, our knowledge tells us that we are also helping them by warning you. Yes, they need help, but you are not the one to give it. Hopefully that idea will make more sense as you read through the book.

We have a lot of empathy for people with high-conflict personalities, because they acquired them in their early years through no choice of their own—often having been born this way or having experienced abuse growing up. Some of them were praised excessively by their parents, which sounds nice until you consider that it promotes self-absorption and sets people up to be unsuccessful in relationships. Because of their trauma or misguided parenting, they need counseling, but they rarely realize it.

So we don't relish the idea of placing warning labels on specific people, and we urge you to keep this kind of thinking to yourself. Even describing them as a group makes us uncomfortable. But after years of conflicted thoughts and feelings, we've concluded that it's our responsibility to share our knowledge and warn you about several personality types that we believe you will regret marrying or committing to. And if you believe you have one of these personality types, we urge you to get counseling to work on overcoming negative behavior patterns and learn how to have more satisfying relationships.

The four high-conflict personality types discussed in this book are narcissistic, borderline, antisocial (sociopathic), and histrionic. We do not mean to suggest that everyone who has one of these personality types is a high-conflict person. Many are not. The key factor for high-conflict people is that they seek and attack *targets of blame*. These are the most difficult of difficult people and truly the kind that will make your life hell, in varying degrees, if you commit to them in any way. The pain and devastation we've seen in divorce and child custody battles has convinced us of the need to warn people *before* they get in these relationships. Children of those with high-conflict personalities are affected for a lifetime, in their physical health and especially in their romantic relationships and parenting. Believe us when we say that you will regret having chosen someone with a high-conflict personality to be the other parent of your children.

Ultimately, it's up to you, but we urge you to use what you learn about dating radar to make the best decision for you and your children or future children. With this knowledge comes power that can be used for good or for bad. Use it wisely, please, in making your own decisions and not publicly labeling individuals.

After you read the story below, you'll have a better sense of the stinging and destructive reality of high-conflict relationships.

Kelly's Story

Kelly and Josh met in college and were instantly attracted to each other. He was on the football team and she was a student intern helping out at football practices. The relationship progressed quickly from a first date to being exclusive in just two weeks. They started doing everything together and even kept in touch during classes through texts and messaging.

It wasn't long before Josh became more controlling of some aspects of their relationship, although the control was subtle. He told her when she could and couldn't attend his football games and who she could and couldn't be friends with. In the beginning, he wanted to spend every second with her, but before long he spent less time with her and more time with other people. He went out with friends whenever he wanted but made her feel bad about spending time with her friends.

She didn't say a word when he was dismissive or critical of her—often in front of their friends. She did his homework for him and picked him up from parties at all times of the night. She would do anything for him, even though he didn't do much for her. Kelly just wanted to be in a relationship. In fact, she felt that she *needed* to have a partner. Josh did, too, but in a different way. He liked showing her off to his friends. Although Kelly didn't seem aware of it, she was willing to go along with whatever he wanted.

It wasn't perfect, but whose relationship is? Once in a while Josh would write sweet love letters to Kelly, which kept her in the game. Within three months she was pregnant, and two months later, just days after their graduation from college, they got married.

The honeymoon was short—just Saturday night and Sunday. On Monday he went back to work and Kelly spent time with her family, who were in town for the wedding. Heading back home after a day of sightseeing with her family, her car broke down on the freeway and, unfortunately, her cell phone was almost dead. She had just enough battery left to call for a tow truck, but then she was stuck with no way to reach Josh. Three hours passed before she was able to reach him, using the tow truck driver's phone.

Kelly explained her situation and apologized profusely. Instead of the understanding and compassion she expected for someone in her situation, especially from the man she'd married just forty-eight hours earlier, Josh's reaction was the complete opposite. He began yelling at her, calling her every foul name in the book and accusing her of cheating on him: "You are a f—ing c— who spreads her legs for every c— that walks by! You whore! Get your ass home! *Now!* I don't care what excuse you have or how you get here, you f—-ing bitch!" It didn't end there; he kept raging for five long minutes while the tow truck driver sat there, trying to pretend he wasn't hearing the tirade.

Shocked, embarrassed, and in tears, she handed the phone back to the driver and began the dreaded trip home. In those few minutes on the phone, Kelly's life took a new direction. After the high of the wedding a couple of days earlier, her life and dreams crashed. She became terrified and obedient, like a beaten dog.

Kelly never told anyone that she always felt like she was walking on eggshells, being careful of what she did and said. Or that she had to wait for permission to go places and talk to certain people. Or that Josh was nice to her in private and demeaning in public. Or that she could tell by the tone he used with her whether someone else was giving him attention—he was nice to her when they weren't, and nasty when they were. Or that she now weighed just 95 pounds, although her normal weight was around 135 pounds.

Kelly and Josh stayed married for a few years and had children, but eventually the bubble burst and she began fighting back, which led to more violence. Divorce wasn't far behind. The ramifications of this seven-year relationship shaped Kelly's future. Her confidence was depleted and her ability to pick a "good" guy in her future relationships was compromised. Some childhood trauma she had never dealt with now had new trauma piled on top of it—all of it affecting her relationships, her self-esteem, and even her career. The relationship with Josh also had negative effects on their children, especially as they began dating in their teen years.

Was this a high-conflict relationship? Was Kelly dealing with a high-conflict person? Yes! What were the indicators? Their moving too fast in the beginning; Josh's uncontrollable anger, rage, violence, and need to control Kelly; her weight loss.

Could Kelly have seen it in the beginning? More on that later. First, more on the true nature of the high-conflict person. (And if you're wondering whether more men or women are high-conflict people, just wait—you'll see that HCPs are an equal-opportunity group).

How Much Conflict Counts As High Conflict?

Every relationship has struggles. When two people live together, they're guaranteed to have different opinions, different points of view, and different ways of doing things. Most couples experience a fair amount of conflict during the first years of marriage, but they navigate it together and eventually settle into a pattern that works for them. Some of these partnerships may eventually end in separation or divorce for a variety of reasons, such as mismatched libido or different hopes when it comes to having children. But many couples remain together and learn to integrate their lives and their individual needs.

The high-conflict relationship is different in its beginning, middle, and end. Why? Because at least one partner comes into it with a high-conflict personality. This is the personality that drives discord, almost as if it needs clashes and drama to feel okay.

The high-conflict partner has a pattern of behavior that eventually surfaces and creates chaos. It usually involves many or all of these:

- Blame (for just about everything)
- Manipulation
- Lying, deceitfulness, conning
- Cognitive distortions
- Controlling
- Dominating
- All-or-nothing thinking (people and situations are either all good or all bad)
- Hitting, biting, throwing, scratching, raging
- Staying stuck in the past
- Cutting people out of their life (or idealizing people in the beginning, then cutting them out later)
- Jumping to conclusions
- Trouble handling feedback or criticism (reacting to many things as criticisms)
- Jealousy of your other relationships
- Indecisiveness
- Defensiveness and contentiousness
- Domestic violence against you or child abuse against your child
- False allegations of domestic violence or child abuse against you
- Divisiveness
- Road rage, jumping out of a moving car
- Depression
- Threatening lawsuits
- Suicide threats

We're talking about the most difficult of difficult relationships—the kind that you'd be afraid to talk about with friends or family because the reality of it sounds absurd, insane, or unreal. Or because it's shameful or embarrassing. Or because you fear harm or retribution from the high-conflict partner.

A Closer Look at the High-Conflict Partner

Someone with a high-conflict personality (HCP) displays these four primary characteristics:

All-or-nothing thinking
Unmanaged emotions
Extreme behavior or threats
Preoccupation with blaming others

Of course, HCPs vary in how extreme these characteristics are, and they can be more or less severe depending on the situation. However, someone with a high-conflict personality has an *ongoing pattern* of these characteristics that eventually stands out. Most people see HCPs as unpredictable, but this pattern actually makes them quite predictable. You'll understand why by the end of this book.

The Big Reveal

People (especially dating partners) are often totally stunned when they first start seeing these patterns. "He was so nice," they say. Or "She was so easygoing!" It's as if another person emerges out of their body. But the reality is that this person was always there, just covered up temporarily by their sugar-coated public persona and ability to fly under their dating partner's radar.

In most relationships the patterns emerge gradually, while in others the transition from wonderful to awful happens overnight. In the introduction to this book, we mentioned our online relationship survey. Throughout the book we will give you some of the results. One part of the survey showed that high-conflict behaviors emerged "overnight" in 11 percent of the couples, "over time" in 39 percent of the couples, and "later in the relationship" for 16 percent of the couples. Most in the "other" category (33 percent) reported their partner changed over a period of a few weeks or months, and in some cases the changes happened years into the relationship.

Q7 Did changes happen (displaying high-conflict behaviors) overnight? Or did the behavior changes occur over time or later in the relationship?

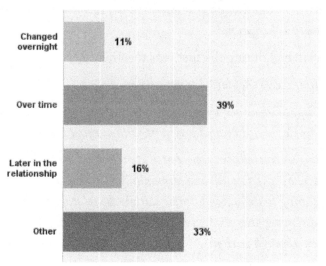

Responses reflected that the change usually happened shortly (sometimes days or weeks) after the relationship was made permanent in some way—such as getting engaged, getting married, or moving in together. For many couples, the change occurred with pregnancy or after the birth of a child.

Here are some quotes from survey comments.

Some saw a major change immediately after committing:

He seemed to change most after our engagement and changed even more dramatically than that immediately after getting married. It was during our honeymoon, those three days following our wedding, that his behavior took a turn for the worse and I realized I'd just made the greatest mistake of my life.

I knew on our honeymoon.

It started on our wedding night. He told me he was on his best behavior while we were dating and now that we were married he could let his true colors show. I thought he was being sarcastic—he was not.

Some switched during the first year together:

Within weeks she started to get very needy.

He flipped about six months into the relationship—then things got worse when I became pregnant with our first child.

Changes occurred over time, but as it progressed she became more and more self-focused and demanding. Within a year I was beginning to feel uncomfortable within the relationship, but my conditioning was that once you commit to a relationship, you follow through with it.

Some took more than a year:

The most obvious changes revealed themselves after the first two years of marriage and with the birth of our two children. The day I was in labor with our first child there was a big change. After that there were small changes until he was in control of all aspects of our lives

After a previous relationship with a sociopath, I waited for three years before I married him. He knew about my shame around divorce, and once we were married his behavior changed significantly. For example, he suddenly became grumpy with me and rude to my children. He also had high expectations of me to bring home the bacon and cook it, and very low expectations of himself. When I finally got up the nerve to question him, he would cross his arms and angrily ask if I wanted him to leave!

After five years together he was forced to admit he had been lying to me about several things. Once that came out into the open he offered no apology but said, basically, "That's just the way I am—I can't change," and stopped doing most everything he had ever done to please me.

And some said they missed signs that were there from the start:

These behaviors were always there. I just didn't realize what was going on until I was totally in love with him.

…always, or perhaps my eyesight changed. I was overlooking, brushing aside, and tolerating what other people do not.

You can see that these changes surprised most of their partners. We just don't expect people to switch like that. But you can also see how deceptive the first few months (or years) can be with an HCP. Some can hide their high-conflict behavior longer than others. But in most cases it shows up within a year—especially if you know what to look for.

Types of High-Conflict Partners

The key is to look for the patterns. High-conflict partners act out in predictable, negative ways in relationships with others. But not all HCPs are alike. In this book, we'll look at four HCP types. Each type has a different core fear that drives their behavior.

Narcissistic HCPs

Narcissistic HCPs have a preoccupation with looking superior to those around them, including (especially) their relationship partners. It's usually not very long before they start trying to show others and the public how superior they are to you. They'll portray you as silly, or stupid, or overemotional, in order to make themselves look so much more reasonable in comparison. Their underlying fear is being seen as inferior or weak (which is how they feel a lot of the time), so they overcompensate by putting you down to build themselves up. You'll learn about narcissistic HCPs in chapter 4.

Borderline HCPs

Borderline HCPs are preoccupied with a fear of abandonment. They need to feel attached to their romantic partners all of the time. So they cling to you by phoning or texting constantly during the day and night, whenever you are away—or even in the same room but absorbed in something else. Even if you're at work or dealing with important matters with others, borderline partners try to intrude to get reassurance that they are still important, too. They struggle when their partner feels too far and, strange as it may seem, they also struggle when their partner is too close. Since their underlying fear is being abandoned, they cling until they feel abandoned (which happens pretty often), then they go into a rage against their partner, repeatedly sabotaging themselves and the relationship. We'll talk about the "love-hate," "Jekyll-Hyde" borderline type HCPs in chapter 5.

Antisocial (Sociopathic) HCPs

Antisocial and sociopath are fairly equivalent terms for this personality. Sociopath is more commonly used in police work and news reporting. Antisocial is more of a mental health term, but that's where the research we have comes from. So we use both terms from time to time. Antisocial HCPs can be extremely charming, masking the reality that they don't really care about anyone but themselves. They use people to get what they want, whether it's money, a prized object, an advantage in a business deal, or access to another person they can dominate. They are always scheming, but denying that they're scheming. "I've never hurt you, so don't be so suspicious," they say, when you actually figure out what they are up to. Their underlying fear is of being dominated by others, so they put lots of energy into preempting that possibility by trying to dominate others— especially their relationship partners. We'll take a closer look at antisocial (sociopath) HCPs in chapter 6.

Histrionic HCPs

Histrionic HCPs can be extremely dramatic and reactive. It's as though they are a pincushion. Everything triggers an extreme emotional response. They react to minor events as if they were national crises, and blame their partners for their anger or pain. "How could you do such a thing? Didn't you realize how upsetting that would be to me? Oh my God!!! You're so incredibly mean and hurtful to me!!!" Maybe you took too long to return a phone call, or forgot to bring something home from the store, or you spent a minute talking to someone your partner doesn't like. The histrionic HCP's underlying fear is of being ignored—of not being the center of attention. If you're in a relationship with someone like this, you will be expected to make them the absolute center of your life. You'll learn more about histrionic HCPs in chapter 7.

Narcissist HCP	Borderline HCP	Sociopath HCP	Histrionic HCP
FEAR OF BEING INFERIOR	FEAR OF BEING ABANDONED	FEAR OF BEING DOMINATED	FEAR OF BEING IGNORED
Demanding Demeaning Self-absorbed Insulting	Overly friendly Shifts to anger Sudden mood swings	Breaks rules & laws Deceptive Con artist	Superficial & helpless Attention-seeking Exaggerates
Needs to be **superior**	Needs to be **attached**	Needs to **dominate**	Needs to be **center of attention**

Other Personal Issues

Beyond these four types, there are some other issues that can lead to a great deal of relationship conflict.

PARANOIA

All of these personality types have a higher-than-average level of paranoia (although individuals vary). They are frequently suspicious of others, including (especially) the people they're in relationships with. They demand to know who you talk to or have lunch with at work, and whether you're sleeping with them, too. They imagine that you and others are conspiring against them. They will demand that you reduce your contacts with their perceived enemies, who may include just about everyone you know. If you have children, they will teach them to spy on you and share their suspicions. Their underlying fear is of being betrayed by those closest to them, and their relationship partner can never be truly trusted. We'll take a closer look at paranoia in chapter 8, along with the following other problems.

BIPOLAR DISORDER

People with bipolar disorder can be similar to those with high-conflict personalities in terms of the ways they affect their partners. Their moods can swing from mania (having high energy, spending money, meeting strangers and bringing them home) to depression (having low energy, secluding themselves for months, not returning phone calls from friends and family). They can be very aggressive, unpredictable, risk-taking, and dramatic. They can also be very charming and exciting.

It's a very confusing situation, once you start to realize that these extreme ups and downs are a pattern. Fortunately, there are medications that can significantly help with the symptoms of bipolar disorder. Unfortunately, people with this disorder often go off their meds, and the relationship can feel like a roller coaster.

ADDICTIONS

Addictions can cause behavior patterns that are much like those of high-conflict personalities, especially in romantic relationships. Moods can be altered by substances, so that highs are exaggerated (especially for people taking stimulants like amphetamines and cocaine) or lows are exaggerated (especially for those taking depressants like alcohol, narcotics, or pain pills such as opioids). Their partners often don't know what is influencing those moods and may even blame themselves—wondering if they did something wrong or if they're going crazy. There may be little or big fights that seemed to start over nothing. When drugs distort reality, the "issue" is usually not the issue. It's the substance abuse that's really the issue.

POST-TRAUMATIC STRESS DISORDER

People who have experienced violent or life-threatening situations (such as child abuse, rape, domestic violence, or combat) may end up with post-traumatic stress disorder (PTSD). For these folks, overreaction in romantic relationships is common. The vulnerability of intimacy combined with the excessive drive to feel safe can trigger confusion and what appear to be personality changes that can last for just minutes, or days or weeks at a time. Again, the "issue" is not the issue. The PTSD may be the issue.

Not all people with these problems—paranoia, bipolar disorder, addictions, and PTSD—have a high-conflict personality. However, people with high-conflict personalities often have one or more of these other problems.

Focus on Fear

HCPs thrive when they are able to control their fears. How do they do this? They use you! The HCP's fears (one or more of the four conflict-driving fears we mentioned in the chart above) require the relationship to be all about them and meeting their fear-based needs.

Their fears are so great that they create ongoing anxiety. When any of us are anxious, we do whatever it takes to not feel anxious. When we feel fear, we take necessary actions to alleviate the fear. Think about your greatest fear. Is it a fear of spiders or snakes? Or maybe it's a fear of heights or flying. Do you feel anxious when confronted with your worst fear? Of course you do. Anxiety is our natural response to fear. If you fear snakes, when you see one you'll do whatever it takes to get away from it and reach safety. Breathe again. Relax.

The core fear of HCPs is navigating relationships, which cause anxiety that they need to escape. For example, when the narcissistic HCP's fear of feeling inferior is triggered, they take action to eliminate the fear. This is why they are so predictable. They immediately do whatever it takes to feel superior again. They do it by putting you down—verbally, emotionally, physically, or sexually. And as soon as they do, they're right back to feeling superior again. The inferior feeling has left the building…at least until the next time the inferiority trigger is activated.

Remember Josh and Kelly? Josh had an underlying fear-based personality, which made him feel anxious most of the time, and he was desperate for relief. When he arrived home after work and his new bride was nowhere to be found, his anxiety button was triggered. Instead of taking a step back to think about potential reasons for her absence, his mind started whirling around one feeling and one thought—he'd been abandoned, dominated, and maybe even made to feel inferior. This wasn't something his operating system could tolerate. He felt bad and had to do whatever it took to get rid of the horrible anxiety. He felt better after unloading his extreme anger and curses on Kelly over the phone.

His verbal vomit had the opposite effect on her, of course. She felt much, much worse, but reluctantly and unwittingly came to accept this behavior as part of the package that she desperately needed. Was it in her best interest to stay with him? Of course not, but past trauma she'd brought into the relationship kept her desperate to hang on to it, although she'd never made that connection in her mind. Josh had no clue about his long-term effect on her or the marriage. Lashing out at Kelly was an automatic and necessary way of getting himself back to normal.

When another person does something, or even has a tone of voice, that isn't appreciated, the HCP's anxiety spikes and they'll do whatever it takes to make it go away. The histrionic HCP, for example, feels like a pincushion. Everything pricks them and triggers a dramatic, emotional overreaction. Drama, drama, drama. They grab your attention and won't let go—until they get their audience's attention and their emotional reaction is exhausted. But the relief only lasts until the next time their drive to be the center of attention is activated again.

In other words, the actions and reactions of HCPs aren't optional, just as their behaviors aren't optional. They're driven by a fear-based personality that started early in life and has been developing since then. Every action they take is an attempt to alleviate their fear of feeling inferior, abandoned, dominated, or ignored. They depend on you to make them feel okay.

Think of it this way: most people can be flexible. Adaptability is a basic skill needed in human relationships—if we're too rigid or uncompromising, we'll end up alone. We realize we have options and that we must give and take to have a healthy partnership.

On the other hand, someone with a high-conflict personality operates on the basis of fear. Fear is their operating system—their infrastructure. The way their brain operates. Everything they perceive and do in relationships, especially romantic relationships, is first and foremost about responding to threats to their vulnerabilities. It's how they operate. But they don't know it—and, probably, neither do we. So we expect them to operate just like we do, and we're surprised when they don't.

Stop being surprised! Adjust your expectations. And whatever you do, *don't tell them they are operating out of fear, or that they have a high-conflict personality!* That would likely just make them angry, and they would need to get even with you just for saying it. Retaliation can last for weeks or months or years.

The Arc of the High-Conflict Relationship

Just as high-conflict people have characteristic patterns, the high-conflict relationship has a predictable trajectory. Of course every relationship is unique, but when it comes right down to it, we know essentially how it starts and how it plays itself out.

The Beginning: Seduction and Salesmanship

Why would anyone want to spend their life with a person who will eventually make them miserable? Most don't, but we get fooled in the beginning because HCPs are great salespeople. Typically, during the attraction phase and the early dating part of the relationship, they are charming, seductive, and fun. They create a feeling of intensity or comfortableness beyond other relationships and we experience this feeling as true love.

Here's why: Almost everyone wants to be in a romantic relationship, but HCPs *need* to be in one just to feel okay. Having a partner is a way to manage the anxiety created by their fear-based operating system. So they make themselves into what we want them to be. They put the best version of themselves—the bling version—out to the public. They're agreeable, compatible, adaptable, flexible, charming, happy, fun, or relaxed. They know how to hook us. And even when their high-conflict personality traits begin to reveal themselves, many of us simply turn a blind eye, out of our own need for connection.

In many relationships with HCPs, there's a spark beyond sparks. Eight out of ten people in our survey reported an immediate or nearly immediate spark upon meeting the person who eventually turned out to be an HCP.

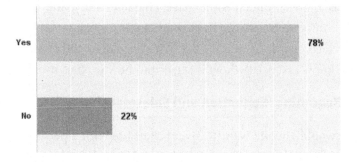

Q4 Did you and your partner have an immediate or nearly immediate spark when you met?

Yes — 78%

No — 22%

Is it any wonder we get hooked? Who wouldn't want that incredible feeling of the intense spark of love? It leads us to believe that we're in for a lifetime of joy. We feel something that we think proves we've found "the one," but that feeling in and of itself is a red flag. The old adage applies: if it's too good to be true, it probably is.

As you saw in the survey comments, the fun can quickly turn into a nightmare. Moving in together, getting engaged, getting married, or getting pregnant often flips a switch within the HCP. It's the Jekyll and Hyde moment, a phenomenon that's hard to explain but present in many HCP relationships.

This is the turning point, the point of no return, the defining moment. We are catapulted into a state of shock, confusion, and disbelief, wondering what happened to our seemingly amazing relationship.

Not all potentially high-conflict relationships have that sizzle and spark at the beginning. Some are more subtle. Still, the grand promises and extravagant lies build up over time, and the result is the same: bait and switch. What you see is not what you get. Your partner is not the person you thought.

The Middle: Fighting Fear

For some, the realization of the new reality creeps in over time—a gradual process that isn't noticed until someone gets hurt, becomes depressed, or suffers some other negative effect. As for others, a disturbing event like a public meltdown, violence, or intense anger switches on the light bulb and illuminates the fact that your sweetie has been replaced by a frightening stranger.

Kelly instantly knew her life had changed. The fairytale was over and her new nightmare of being controlled and fearful had begun. Depression, dangerous weight loss, and violence—any of which could have been fatal—were the ultimate result.

So what keeps rational people there? Why do we stay in these relationships? This is where our own fear factors in to the equation. We may stay because we fear retribution or harm from our partner if we leave, or out of fear of being single and lonely or embarrassed.

It seems that some are able to rise above it and manage the relationship, but not without some personal sacrifice. Others make adjustments to avoid angering their HCP partner. After the shock wears off, it may feel as if there's no choice but to adapt to this new way of life, this new person. So they walk on eggshells and become a modified version of themselves. Others fight back.

People also want to feel hopeful that their partner will change or that they can help their partner become a better person. They make excuses for bad behavior and live with it until they realize that their hopes are delusional. Or they feel empathy for the partner, which motivates them to stick around longer than they should. And some are just in plain denial, refusing to admit anything is wrong with the partner or with the relationship. Regardless of the reason, it's possible to spend many agonizing years in a state of constant or near-constant fear.

The End: Driven to Destruction

It isn't surprising that HCP relationships are damaging, given that both partners are in a continual state of fear and conflict. After years of being yelled at, demeaned, hit, controlled, and manipulated, and feeling as if the life has been sucked out of them, some people have finally had enough and end the relationship. This often follows an arrest after a big fight, an unforgivable lie that has been exposed, or an affair that has come to light. Something causes such shocking disruption that the choice is made easier.

Some people drift right into the loving arms of another partner—someone who doesn't behave the same way. Others unexpectedly find themselves behaving much like their partner. They blow up, yell, or hit, or react in more internal ways like depression, withdrawal, and isolation. They're shocked by their own behavior and an out-of-control life. Their responses have become reactions and are far outside the way they normally handle themselves.

Even when we know our high-conflict partner's behavior isn't reasonable, we convince ourselves that they will change. But they don't—at least most of them won't. And for those who do, it's only with long-term specific therapy or treatments. Even then, your life and your needs will be put on hold and you will have to exercise warrior-like discipline to live a balanced, happy life.

Sadly, some people lose custody of their children to high-conflict exes. And in the most extreme cases, the final chapter of the relationship may be murder or suicide.

Why Are Some People Like This?

People's personalities are a combination of at least four factors:

- the genetics and temperament they are born with
- their early childhood upbringing
- traumas they may have experienced growing up
- the culture they are born into

Genetics appears to be the basis of 40 percent to 80 percent of someone's personality, depending on the person. Just as you don't pick your natural body shape, hair, and skin color, your personality starts out developing before you are even born. For example, some people are naturally extraverted. They like to talk a lot and are comfortable talking to strangers. Other people are born introverts, who are more reserved and quiet much of the time.

These are just two characteristics people may have from birth. Although these qualities have nothing to do with being a high-conflict person or not, they are a good example of inborn traits.

But what happens as someone grows up can make a big

difference. Just as some introverts become more outgoing and some extraverts become more contemplative, some people with inherited high-conflict traits may soften as they grow up with good parenting. Likewise, some people with slight high-conflict tendencies may grow up in violent or hostile families and become fully high-conflict by adulthood.

Early childhood attachment may be the next most important factor. Ideally, an infant has parents who love and nurture them from the start of life. By providing a balance of soothing reassurance and encouragement for independent exploration, parents can create a sense of security their children. From this attachment, children develop self-confidence, a sense of security in relationships, and the ability to manage and regulate their own emotions.

When children don't develop secure attachment early in life, they may grow up feeling insecure, anxious, or dismissive of normal relationships. Insecure attachments are a risk factor for developing adult personality disorders, which disrupt their relationships because they're unable to see their own contribution to the problems. They will work against their own self-interest, not recognizing that they are creating problems in their relationships and acting in self-defeating ways.

Childhood traumas may also play a role in creating a high-conflict personality. Child abuse, especially when perpetrated by a family member, can have a devastating effect on a child. Abuse comes in many forms: physical, emotional, verbal, and sexual. Even being exposed to parental conflict can be a form of abuse. When traumatized children grow up, their adult relationships may be dominated by manipulation, anger, and lack of trust. The very things that helped them survive in an extremely dysfunctional family can lead them to develop a high-conflict personality.

Some types of childhood trauma are frequently seen in people who develop specific personality disorders. For instance, child sex abuse may be linked to borderline personality disorder (BPD). However, not everyone who has experienced sexual abuse develops this type of personality, and not everyone with BPD was sexually abused as a child. When it comes to personality problems, there is a wide range of causes and effects.

Growing up with a sense of entitlement may also contribute to a high-conflict personality. These are the *"everyone gets a trophy"* or *"everything must be fair"* kids, or those who aren't taught to earn their way in life. In these circumstances, children may come to believe that they are special and will gain things in life without working for them. They can grow up into very self-centered adults, people who are unlikely to form healthy love relationships. No one wants romantic partners who care only about themselves.

Lastly, the culture you grow up in influences your personality development as well, combined with all the other factors. In today's culture, there are more images than ever before of bad behavior—domestic violence, child abuse, disrespect, selfishness, and so forth—and these images become part of our potential behavior. For adults, extreme behavior is a kind of entertainment. But for children growing up, entertainment figures serve as role models, representing normal adult behavior. Likewise, the reduction of face-to-face contact as we live more through texting and social media seems to undermine people's sense of security and personal confidence. We don't know the long-term impact on personality development of all these rapid changes, but indications are that they are contributing to an increase in the development of high-conflict personalities.

How Bad Does It Get?

Of course, not all HCPs are the worst of the worst. All of these characteristics have a range in terms of severity. Any given person may show all or only some of the characteristics of an HCP. They may have a little bit of a tendency toward a trait, or they may have it in spades.

It might be easiest to think of HCPs as being like a Thai food menu. A dish can be mild, medium, spicy, or nuclear. The spicier the dish, the more your mouth will burn. HCPs are the same. Some have a mild or medium level of high-conflict behaviors, and with these folks, you may have a chance at relationship success if you're willing to put in some work. But the people with high levels of high-conflict behaviors are like the spicy and nuclear dishes that come with a warning. Copious amounts of water or ice will be needed to cool the burning. You might be able to choke down the food, but you are not going to enjoy the meal.

Some high-conflict people have such extreme characteristics that they can be diagnosed with personality disorders. Personality disorders are fairly common, but they are nowhere near as well-known as other types of mental illness—such as depression, anxiety, bipolar disorder, substance use disorder, and schizophrenia. The *Diagnostic and Statistical Manual of Mental Disorders*, or *DSM-5*, is the reference book mental health professionals use to make their diagnoses. There are ten personality disorders identified in the *DSM-5*, and they all seem to share some common characteristics:

- The person has a narrow range of dysfunctional behavior, which they repeat and repeat. Every day is Groundhog Day.
- They don't reflect on themselves and their own behavior. That is, they have zero insight.
- They don't change their own behavior. ("Why change? I don't have a problem!")
- It's generally a lifetime condition. It develops in early childhood and lasts until, as they say in the life insurance industry, "plan ends." (There are exceptions, especially with those who have sought treatment for Borderline Personality Disorder.)
- They do not know they have this condition, and you can't make them see it. No matter what you say or do, you won't convince them. This is not a failure on your part; it is one of the defining conditions of a personality disorder.

If you combine these characteristics with the patterns of high-conflict personalities (all-or-nothing thinking, unmanaged emotions, extreme behaviors, and a preoccupation with blaming others), you can see how they will wreak chaos in your life—and keep doing it! Not every personality disorder comes with high-conflict traits, but four or five of the ten typically do.

Simply put, the traits of these disorders include:

A lack of self-awareness
An inability to manage their own emotions
An inability to change their behavior
A pattern of blaming forces outside of themselves

In other words, these people are really stuck in a narrow range of behavior, which is what leads to conflict in their relationships. They tend to blame others, so they are not open to any feedback from their partner—or anyone else. Instead, they become increasingly defensive in the relationship, and therefore conflicts increase, rather than getting resolved. If we're watching out for our own best interest while dating a nuclear HCP, we end the relationship. If we're not, we make excuses for or ignore their behavior and convince ourselves that they will change once we do what they want us to do. We adapt our wants and needs to accommodate them and to avoid living in exhausting chaos.

Medications do not "fix" these personalities. Because they are not "chemical" imbalances or abnormalities, drugs are not used to treat them—although some people are prescribed antianxiety, antipsychotic, or antidepressant medications to reduce anxiety or other symptoms.

Why You Wouldn't Want to Partner with an HCP

The reasons for avoiding marrying or committing to an HCP are surely obvious as you're reading this. So who would voluntarily marry an HCP? Well, think about it: if 10 to 15 percent of divorce and child custody cases are high-conflict battles, *someone* is voluntarily partnering with them.

Even if you're smart, you could end up with an HCP if you don't understand their personalities and behavior patterns, and if you don't watch for the signs. Their initial charm and compatibility trick us into thinking that they're "the one." In many high-conflict relationships, there's an immediate spark that's so intense that it becomes our blind spot. We mistakenly believe (or feel) that the intensity of the spark is the stamp of approval on our "soul mate." Instead, we should think of it as a potential red flag. In non-HCP relationships, the spark is a good sign. With HCPs, it's the opposite.

After convincing you they're awesome in the beginning, HCPs eventually create chaos and conflict. In fact, they seem unsatisfied in its absence. Their partners are miserable. Countless people come to us for consultations in which they pour out their misery. We hear the same words repeated over and over: "I *dread* going home." "I've looked the devil in the eye and lived to tell about it." "I'm exhausted." "My life is chaos." "You won't believe the nightmare I'm living." "I fear for my life." "I fear for my kids' lives." "I'm in a deep, dark hole with no escape." "He will turn the kids against me forever." "I don't even know who I am anymore." "I'm stuck."

Is it possible to see it coming? That's what the rest of this book is about. There are warning signs. You just need to develop your radar and keep it from getting jammed, know what patterns to look for, and learn to overcome your blind spots.

CHAPTER TWO

What Jams Your Radar?

A thousand relationship books, matchmakers, fortune-tellers, and philosophers around the world, and even the most sophisticated dating sites haven't been entirely successful at predicting who will be the best love match. Nor at predicting who will be a *horrible* match. Even when we get good advice, some of us ignore it and leave the future to chance.

Most of the time that's okay, but 10 to 20 percent of the time it isn't, and we end up in relationship hell. You may think that HCPs are from other parts of the world, country, or city, or that you're not going to meet them in the bars you frequent, or that dating sites successfully weed them out. Au contraire. This is an *equal opportunity* personality type. It pays no attention to whether the person is tall or short, skinny or heavy, black or white, rich or poor, high IQ or low IQ, German or Argentinian, Christian or atheist, athlete or book nerd. It can strike anyone anywhere.

High-conflict personalities clearly spell dating disaster. So, how and why *do* we get into relationships with HCPs? If we're an intelligent species, how do we end up picking people who are eventually going to make us regret the day we met them?

In the previous chapter, we told you about four primary characteristics of HCPs:

- All-or-nothing thinking
- Unmanaged emotions
- Extreme behavior or threats
- Preoccupation with blaming others

You'd think these characteristics would be obvious, but that's not necessarily the case. And they can be covered up for a long time. In other words, your radar can be jammed! How does this happen? How can someone be so appealing and at the same time so deceptive?

Attraction, Chemistry, and "the Spark"

Most of us think we can tell—through our feelings, or through attraction and chemistry—whether someone is okay to marry or not. However, that's only part of the picture, and this is where we get caught off guard.

Who can say exactly what attraction is? We may be drawn to a beautiful face, a big chest, curvy hips, six-pack abs, a bald head, stunning intelligence, a sports car, a beautiful home, whatever. Attraction is a helpful component for long-lasting love, but it also may be the thing that scrambles our radar. It's a good start, but it's just one variable in the equation. We need to be sure we're thinking, not just feeling.

The idea that you have "amazing chemistry" or a "mind-blowing spark" should raise a red flag and remind you to pay attention. It might be a positive, but only if the person isn't an HCP. If the chemistry is super strong, there's a good chance it'll be a negative, because it may mean this person is an HCP.

Survey respondents affirmed our theory that there's an intense spark present in many cases during the first stages of what will eventually turn out to be high-conflict relationships.

Eighty percent reported feeling that "spark," an intensity not present in the first stages of other romantic relationships. This seems like an extraordinarily high percentage. While we didn't compare this result to couples without HCP partners, it certainly seems different from the stories we hear from many happy couples, who never had an explosive attraction at the beginning, but grew deeper and deeper in love over time.

Of course, this spark does not automatically mean, on its own, that you are dealing with a high-conflict person. It may not indicate any problem at all. But it does seem to be present in a high percentage of high-conflict cases. So if you feel that spark, that's a warning sign, telling you to look closely at your dating partner and take your time in developing this relationship while watching out for all the other warning signs.

At the risk of bursting your bubble, we'd like to suggest that it may in fact be brain chemistry, not a cosmic event, that creates this intense "spark." Once the reaction is underway, we're in. It's an incredible feeling, beyond just being in love…it's *beyond* beyond. Our heart says *yes, yes, yes!* Our gut says *more, more, more! This is so right!* But we are in danger of missing important cues, because our fact-finding brain is asleep.

The Power of Desperation

Attraction isn't the only thing that makes us vulnerable to HCPs. Desperation can play a role, too.

Maybe you've had a friend who seemed desperate to get married—so desperate that they're willing to risk the high likelihood of divorce rather than listen to reason and call off, or at least put off, the wedding. Thanks to the advent of wedding shows on TV, some people are in love with the idea of a big blowout wedding, one they may not be able to afford, and one that is as good as or better than their friend's wedding. In the swirl of Vera Wang dresses and buttercream icing, it's easy to forget that in the months and years after the wedding, they'll be married to the spouse, not the dress, the cake, or the fabulous honeymoon.

Then there are those who watch their friends walk down the aisle while marriage for them remains elusive. They become desperate to get married to avoid becoming an "old maid" or confirmed bachelor.

And then there are the divorced set and the widows and widowers in the second half of life. Life without a partner can seem pretty bleak. Loneliness creeps in, and maybe fear about one's financial future. Together, these feelings can lead to desperation to find someone—anyone.

In the past two decades, we've observed a diminishment of confidence when it comes to relationships. More people than ever before seem desperate to connect romantically. Maybe it's because they grew up with only one or both parents who were emotionally unavailable or locked in conflict, leaving them yearning for connection. People have always and will always have a desire to connect. It's how we're wired. But at this time in history, a desperation to connect prevails, and we often have to navigate it without much help from family—or society.

At the same time, we don't have much faith that we'll succeed at romance. The divorce rate of our parents' generation has diminished trust in the construct of marriage. Those rates have decreased over the last decade, but only because marriage rates have also gone down. The numbers don't translate to greater relationship stability.

This combination of desire and doubt creates a sort of desperation that works against our self-interest. This is dangerous and leaves us so vulnerable. We take almost everyone at face value, literally. Swipe left, swipe right. You accept someone based wholly on looks, and then you trust their words. Online dating is okay, but only if your relationship radar is fully operational. You need a system in your brain that warns against people who aren't good for you.

What Qualities Attract Us to HCPs?

We asked our survey respondents what attracted them to the person who turned out to be high-conflict. We theorized that charm, compatibility, and adaptability would score high, so we weren't entirely surprised to find that 80 percent listed "charming" as a quality that attracted them, 70 percent listed "compatibility," and 40 percent listed adaptability. Let's look at why these qualities may jam your radar.

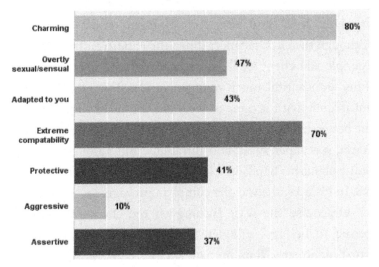

Q6 **What were the qualities that attracted you?**

Charming — 80%
Overtly sexual/sensual — 47%
Adapted to you — 43%
Extreme compatability — 70%
Protective — 41%
Aggressive — 10%
Assertive — 37%

Charm

Think about it. By definition, charm is engaging. Energetic. It makes us feel special. It's all positive. It can sweep us off our feet. Charm triggers lots of powerful, happy emotions inside of us. It makes us feel good about ourselves and helps us forget about all our other worries. It's very seductive—in every way.

But think further about it. Charm is something that a person can turn on or off. When someone really wants something, they can turn on the charm. Think about a child who really, really wants his mom to let him play a game on his tablet. He can turn on the charm before mom can blink, and just as quickly turn it off once he's been turned down or given permission. Interestingly, HCPs really, really want relationships on *their* terms. Yet they often start out by giving the impression that they want a relationship on *your* terms. "What would you like? I'll get it for you." "Where do you want to go? I'll take you there!"

Our clients have told many stories of the charm that first lured them into an eventually high-conflict relationship. Although the circumstances differ, the pattern is the same. One example is a client we'll call Sam, a divorced man who had a thing for beautiful, much younger blondes. That was his criteria, but if along with it came a sweet girl complete with charm, all the better. In his most recent failed relationship, the young lady, Alexa, was super sweet and flirtatious, and flattered him with praise about his handsome looks, his huge "guns," and his Audi R8. In his eyes, she was the complete package.

Of course she was. Turning on the charm, she adapted herself to be "his" complete package. Later, she became his worst nightmare. More on Sam later.

Here are some comments from the survey respondents:

He was Prince Charming, my white knight in shining armor!

He blended well with my family. Charmed the pants off of them. Vowed to take great care of me and to love me like a man should. Basically, told my parents exactly what they wanted to hear, and me, too!

She seemed to really be interested in me and everything about me. She focused in on me with laser-like intensity. I was thrilled because she made me feel that I was very special, and that I was very important to her.

He was a complete charmer during those five months of dating. He bought me gifts and took me on expensive dates. I found out after we were married that he couldn't afford any of those things.

Extremely Compatible with You and Adaptable to You

It's natural to want to get together with someone with whom we have many things in common. It's great when we have the same interests, we look at things the same way, or we share some of the same background, lifestyle, faith, politics, and so forth. There are infinite ways in which people can feel compatible.

Yet we need to think about this further, too. Is the person really compatible, or have they figured out what your interests are and told you stories that match yours? Are your interests really shared, or is your date just saying that they're shared? Do you really have similar backgrounds, lifestyles, faith, sleep patterns, politics, and love for dogs, or is this person making it seem that you do? Are they emphasizing the compatibilities and papering over the incompatibilities—at least for now? In other words, is it fake compatibility?

And how about adaptability? Yes, we all need to be flexible and adapt to our partners and vice versa, but HCPs are overly adaptable in the beginning and just the opposite later in the relationship. Again, are they over-the-top flexible? Are they too accommodating to be real? In other words, is it fake adaptability?

Let's continue with Sam. When he met Alexa across the counter at the bar, he knew nothing about her other than she was hot and made the best margaritas. They chatted. He told her he'd grown up in Santa Fe, New Mexico, that he loved Formula One racing, and especially that he adored his son and his Great Dane. Wasn't he pleasantly surprised when she exclaimed that Santa Fe was one of her favorite places! She'd been a fan of Formula One racing forever! And she just loved kids and dogs—especially Great Danes.

Now, it's not much of a stretch to believe that many people love kids and dogs and car racing, but what you find with HCPs—at first—is an absolute compatibility with most things. When Sam said he was a morning person, wasn't it a miracle that so was she? When he said he'd like to start going to church, what a coincidence that she'd been thinking the same thing! Although compatibility is what we all want in a relationship, apparent matching in almost every way is a red flag indicating that further time and exploration is warranted. In Sam's case, he later found that most of their supposed similarities were as fake as fake news.

Here's a sampling of what survey respondents said on the subject of compatibility:

It seemed that she was the perfect partner—always supportive and easy to get along with.

The person initially, for a short time, seemed to take interest in things that were important to me or close to me. The interest quickly changed after the relationship had solidified.

With made up stories he "marketed" himself well. He found out what I valued and he really became that…until he decided not to anymore. Over years the stories started to not make sense.

It took no effort for me to gain his immediate agreement to things that were important to me but that other people I had dated were unable to be flexible about.

Agreed quickly to change a few habits that I could not live with—told me it was no big deal, those habits meant nothing to her. Years later found out she had been lying about complying.

Overt Sexuality/Sensuality

Who doesn't go for passion and vitality? We love being turned on and excited, especially if it's been a while. These days, there are few social restraints to discourage us from having a physical relationship right at the start, or very early in dating.

This is where chemistry really does play a part. Scientists tell us that the brain is the largest sex organ and that chemicals— such as dopamine, oxytocin, and endorphins—are released before and during sex that keep us coming back for more (Doidge 2007). So even just a hookup can trigger falling in love. Our body chemistry wants us to fall in love *now*, rather than waiting a year to see if this is really the right partner. It's not easy overcoming these powerful drives.

So how do you know if the date who wants to go fast sexually is an HCP or not? It's not easy to tell, at least in the beginning, but it is another red flag to consider. Some HCPs send mixed messages, such as using overt sexuality to flirt with you but then closing the door when you've given in. The opposite can be true, too. They may say they're not the type to have sex on the first date, and then do exactly that with you.

As old-fashioned as this may sound, it really is best to wait awhile and get to know your romantic interest before letting it go all the way. Sex has its place and time in a relationship. Too early can be a warning sign. With some HCPs, sex equals divine connection and you'll have a hard time getting them to disconnect with you once you've discovered they're an HCP.

One of the most common things people tell us, looking back on how they got together with an HCP partner, is how fast the relationship developed—including physically. We have heard countless stories about how the power of sex and sensuality kindled relationships with HCPs, and sometimes led people to compromise their careers, families, or positions in their community or place of worship.

Great sex can also make it hard to split up with an HCP partner, even when all the negatives have become obvious. In other relationships, the sex ends, or gets used as a weapon, once the relationship starts to seem permanent.

Sam brought Alexa home the night they met, even though he had no intention of doing anything with her. She'd confused him all evening. She was suggestive and flirtatious—short skirt, tight shirt, cleavage bursting. She oozed sensuality but in a shy way. She told him that she didn't believe in having sex on a first date, so he was pleasantly surprised when he walked her to her car and she started kissing him passionately and pressing herself against him. She no longer seemed resistant to the idea of sex on a first date, so what the heck! The next morning he was fixing breakfast in bed (his) for her.

Throughout their relationship Alexa used sex to get her way. At the end, he couldn't get her out of his house until he literally deposited her on her family's doorstep.

Here's a sampling of what survey respondents said about sex and sensuality in their HCP relationships:

Funny, caring, extremely sexual, charming.

She gave the impression that she was a good church girl who didn't sleep around. In fact, she outright said it during dinner, but later began kissing and groping me, and begged me to take her to my place. So I did.

One month after our first date, he just started coming around every night.

Protectiveness

Protectiveness is a powerful quality if you are looking for someone to rescue you from your past (an abusive childhood or other traumatic experiences) or even your present (a recent or current bad relationship, for example). Isn't this the idea of romance that we were taught from very early childhood? Prince Charming! A movie star wife! Someone will fall into our lives and sweep us off our feet. They will keep us from harm and fix everything that has ever been broken. This is what Hollywood and soap operas are made of.

Our part in this process—our blind spots—we will talk about in the next chapter. But here we're talking about HCPs who *act* protective but won't really be that way once you're hooked.

Here are some survey comments about charm and protectiveness:

Took care of me and provided for me in ways my family never did.

I couldn't shake her, and mistook things like stalking for love. Sometimes protective. It was the initial dream of how well she treated me in the beginning that I hoped would come back.

This person had that "Prince Charming" quality. He wanted to take care of me and be my knight in shining armor. When the dust settled and the honeymoon was over I was faced with a mentally disturbed and violent man with a very violent and abusive past. These types of men are master manipulators and pathological liars.

Other Attractive Qualities of HCPs

Our survey showed "assertive" (37%) as an attracting quality and, to a much lesser extent, "aggressive" (10%). Assertive people garner respect, especially from those who have a hard time being assertive themselves. Assertiveness tends to open doors, and that can be impressive. So attraction to assertiveness is easy to understand, but why the attraction to aggression? Frankly, it's a turn-on to some. Power, strength, might, bravado. These can be enticing if you get a kick out of someone who gets in your face, or threatens to hurt the guy in the next lane who just cut you off. Unlike the "fake" nature of compatibility, adaptability, or protectiveness, the attracting qualities of assertiveness and aggressiveness have a "real" nature. Attraction to aggressive people may seem surprising, but there you have it.

Survey participants also wrote in additional details about the qualities that attracted them to their HCP partner. Common responses were:

- Highly intelligent (most often mentioned)
- Extremely caring and gentle
- Kind, considerate, and caring
- Gentle personality and easygoing
- Shared faith and interests
- Intelligence, appearance, physical attraction
- Interest in similar activities
- Generous, funny, exciting, passionate
- Similar lifestyles and approach to the day
- Lonely and vulnerable
- Life of the party
- Sensitive, adoring, supportive, easy to get along with
- Financially secure, organized, successful
- Shared common commitment to a cause or faith
- Athletic
- Took care of me, took interest in me, was there for me all the time
- Honest and honorable and trustworthy
- Made me a priority; understanding, loved everything about me
- Very romantic, anticipated my needs, love-bombed me

What's striking about this list is that these are also common terms people use to describe how their healthy and happy relationships began. Many couples who have been good together for 20 or 30 or 40 years say the same things. So consider these yellow warning signs that call for caution, not necessarily red labels telling you to avoid at all costs.

When we have helped people going through divorce from a high-conflict person, sometimes they tell us "There are two Williams," or "There are two Marys." Many people who know them only know the charming, easygoing, considerate one. Neighbors and acquaintances say the person is "such a nice guy," or she was "just a regular girl next door." But then again, people often say these things during criminal investigations in the news. People can fool us by seeming to be just like us. Keep in mind, there may be another William or Mary that's being kept out of sight while you're dating, who may be boorish, selfish, or mean.

So how can you sort out those who put on a good act and jam your radar? As one of the people commented above, her partner was "marketing" himself to her. Just as you can learn to spot a slick sales pitch, you can tune your dating radar to screen out the folks who are trying to fool you.

Don't Let Them Jam Your Radar

Here are three strategies to help keep an HCP from jamming your radar:

1. Maintain a Healthy Skepticism

Awareness is key. Stay alert, and keep just enough distance to retain your perspective. The problem most of us have is being too trusting and believing that everyone is okay, that everyone is like us, or that people who should be avoided come with a sign. They don't.

Because of their fear-driven behavior, HCPs are on their best behavior when meeting potential romantic partners.

Remember, the deception is not intentional. Most of them are not out to harm you or make your life hell. They don't even know they operate this way. And many of them are pretty miserable, but they don't know why, and they honestly believe or feel that a relationship is the only fix for their misery.

So maintain a healthy skepticism. *This is a powerful and essential first step.* So many people don't even realize how common this HCP "best behavior" can be—at least until they've been burned once, or more.

Don't overlook warning signs. Check them out in your mind, and talk them through with people you trust. Sometimes, you'll perceive the warning signs in your own responses to the person rather than in their behavior. Here's what we were told in the survey:

Listen to your instincts. My gut told me something was off, though I could not put my finger on it. So I dismissed it. I listen to my instincts now.

Respect your own judgment and how your body feels. If you're feeling anxious, have stomachaches, are constantly stressed or always defending your own reasonable behavior, get out.

Do listen to the doubts of friends and family. They can see things that you are blind to!

Don't get involved before you know them. Watch how they are with others. Don't show interest until you know you are interested. And if you see traits that concern you, don't get involved.

We wouldn't go so far as to say "don't show interest," but we agree with the idea of watching how they are with others. You can show interest, but stop short of making major commitments like moving in together, loaning money, having a baby, starting a business together, merging bank accounts, adopting a rescue dog together, getting engaged or married—anything that has a permanent or somewhat permanent quality to it—until you know the person well.

2. Watch for Extremes

Notice how common "extremely compatible" was (70% in our survey) as a quality that hooked partners in? This should put you on the alert. How about "extremely caring and gentle?" These all may be totally true, and if they are that's a good thing. But you should observe these traits over time, with a healthy skepticism, before concluding that they are not phony deceptions jamming your radar.

Just put "extremely" in front of the four highest-rated qualities to watch out for:

Extremely charming
Extremely compatible
Extremely sexual/sensual
Extremely protective

This will help you be more aware of possible deception. Listen to how you describe the person to your friends. Is it with extremes? Do your friends seem a little bit skeptical? How do you respond if they say, "He sounds too good to be true" or "She sounds too perfect"? Are you defensive or reflective? If you can say, "I'll keep my eyes open," you're probably taking a healthy approach.

Also, watch out for people who seem extremely attached or expect extreme togetherness. It's common at first in a relationship to spend lots of time together. But you need to know whether or not the person has the ability to spend time away from you without falling apart. Otherwise, you may be dealing with an HCP who will do an extremely good job of taking over your life if you let them, and you will have an extremely hard time getting them out of your life. This has often happened in high-conflict cases we see.

Some survey comments supporting concerns about extremes:

Seek someone that can support themselves and has some independence.

Pick the person with whom you have chemistry on a scale of about 5–7 out of 10. Do not date someone who you feel 10/10 chemistry with—this is your imago and you should stay away. ["Imago" is Harville Hendrix's term for a fantasy type from childhood—often created from familiar negative experiences.]

3. Take Your Time

High-conflict people generally want to move fast. Overall, they seem more impatient than the average person. Perhaps they simply have more anxious or aggressive energy because they tend to be off balance and have trouble regulating their own emotions. Or maybe they realize that you will find out who they are and they want to get a commitment from you before that happens. Many of our survey respondents mentioned that the big change from extremely positive to extremely negative came soon after they got engaged, married, or pregnant, or had a child.

In general, speed is a factor to watch out for more than almost any other. It's the biggest, reddest red flag. We recommend that you wait at least a year before getting married or planning to have a child. Getting engaged, however, could be a good move, as long as it's a long engagement. Being engaged for a year or more may actually make things clearer before you take on larger commitments, as many survey respondents said the high-conflict personality came out after "the relationship solidified" or after getting engaged or living together. The idea is to make sure that time is on your side in seeing deeper into the person's full range of personality patterns and behavior.

Here's what some of the survey respondents had to say:

Beware the overtly strong, over-the-top devotion if it shows itself almost immediately. Don't trust words—trust actions.

Do not compromise your values. No sexual relationship for as long as possible.

You really don't know a person until you've seen them in all four seasons (fall, winter, spring, summer). That means it will be at least a year before you do.

Date a long time, over a year. Don't give up your life, family, or friends.

Some survey respondents advised waiting even two or three years before getting married or having children, but that may not be realistic for many people. Waiting at least one year should be adequate for most situations, so long as you have eyes wide open and don't let your radar get jammed. From our experience in dealing with high-conflict individuals, their patterns usually show up within a year—if you know what to look for.

Applying these Strategies to Relationship Stages

So, how do you identify an HCP before it's too late? You must pay attention before your heart goes all in. Use the dating radar you are developing to pick up the signals. This means staying skeptical, watching carefully for extremes, and allowing enough time for your partner to show their true colors.

We'll cover the telltale signs at two relationship stages. Slow down and proceed with caution if any of these signs are present, even if it's only one or two.

In the beginning...

The beginning stages (the first six months) of a relationship are the most critical time for spotting HCP warning signs. As you fall in love, your brain is awash in dopamine, oxytocin, and endorphins, screaming that it feels so good. It takes a serious commitment to see clearly through the cloud of love sparkles. You have to override these powerful emotional forces and pay attention to the logical part of your mind. You have to be sure that your heart doesn't overwhelm your brain.

The following are signs to watch for in the beginning stages.

What the other person does to jam your radar:

- Gets very close very soon
- Is extremely sexual or sensual
- Is available for everything, all the time
- Shows complete or near complete compatibility with what you want to do, where you want to go, and so on
- Talks of multiple past relationships
- Blames everyone else for relationship problems
- Talks about past childhood abuse too soon

What you feel:

- Intense spark
- Racing heart
- Mushy inside

- Exploding stars above your head
- Wanting to help them
- Amazing connection
- Extreme sexual attraction

Over Time...

Here are the some signs to watch for while dating over time.

What the other person does (revealing more of themselves):
- Love-bombs you
- Wants to get married or move in together—fast!
- Has no boundaries (shares your intimate life details with others, for example)
- Has rigid boundaries (refuses to let you see their friends, family)
- Explodes and then apologies
- Explodes and doesn't apologize
- Manipulates you (or other people)
- Reacts defensively
- Lies
- Argues; provokes confrontation
- Tells stories that don't match reality
- Tries to control you (or other people)
- Behaves abusively
- Curses at you
- Puts you down in some personal way (looks, weight, education, intelligence)
- Rages
- Asks you to lie for them
- Threatens suicide if you leave
- Accuses you of the actions they're actually doing

- Checks your email, phone, social media, everything (and accuses you of doing it)
- Harasses you
- Stalks you
- Damages your property in any way
- Is violent toward you or your children
- Is indecisive; wants you to make decisions, then thwarts them
- Behaves inflexibly
- Flip-flops on many things
- Other extreme (outside the norm) behaviors or actions

What you feel:
- Confusion about their stories
- Confusion about your feelings
- A gut feeling that something isn't right
- Dread at the thought of seeing them
- Fear
- A need to hide things about yourself (feelings, likes and dislikes)
- Anger toward them, far outside your norm
- A need to apologize a lot
- As if you can't do anything right
- As if you're walking on eggshells
- A compulsion to lie so you don't get "in trouble"
- A need to hide the truth from family and friends

At the End...

Be aware that these are potential HCP behaviors when the relationship ends (regardless of which person initiates it).

What the other person does (revealing full potential of themselves):

- Yells and screams at you
- Spreads rumors about you
- Makes false allegations against you to friends and family
- Attempts to persuade your family to criticize your actions or turn against you
- Recruits others (including your former friends) to bad-mouth you to others
- Makes disparaging remarks about you to your children, or tries to turn them against you
- Becomes violent with you or threatens you with violence
- Threatens to expose your secrets
- Releases revenge porn on social media
- Goes to court to obtain court orders against you (restraining orders, child custody limitations, and so on)
- Sabotages your reputation at your job
- Falsely accuses you of violence or abuse, causing you to end up in jail or losing access to your children
- Holds you against your will
- Interferes in your future relationships
- Stalks you

What you feel:
- Terrified
- Isolated; cut off from friends and family
- As if you're walking on eggshells
- Repeatedly caught by surprise at your former partner's hostile behavior
- Shocked at the hostility of others your former partner has recruited

- Confused about sudden court involvement in your life
- Angry about court interference in your relationship with your children
- Fearful of financial ruin
- Stuck; frozen

How HCPs Jam Your Radar: Two Extreme Examples

Some high-conflict relationships are so volatile that someone ends up dead. A partner who engages in extreme violence is probably also going to do a very thorough job of jamming your radar. If you know what to look for, you can see this in the news reporting on these cases.

The Millionaire and the Escort

Peter Morgan, a millionaire and married father of two in Wales, was brought to trial for the death of Georgina Symonds, his paid personal escort, who was found strangled to death in early 2016. After first denying he'd killed her, he later admitted he had.

Court records and testimony indicated that he'd paid her to stop seeing other men and had lavished her with expensive gifts like helicopter rides, expensive cars, and spa days; paid her an escort fee of up to £10,000 per month; gave her a bungalow to live in (with her young son); and promised she'd receive £1 million from a life insurance policy upon his death.

Morgan explained in his testimony that when they met, "... George [Georgina] said to me 'My heart's racing' and I said 'So is mine.' She said, 'Did you feel that? It feels like love to me.'" Within a few days, their relationship turned sexual.

In testimony to the court, her best friend, Alexy Butcher, testified that Symonds was grieving the death of a past boyfriend when she met Morgan. She was "very depressed" over the death of her ex-boyfriend, turned to drugs and alcohol, and "tried to take her own life," Butcher said. Morgan "was helping her with her grief as much as he could but she blamed him. She wasn't very nice to him," she added.

Over time, Peter Morgan became increasingly controlling and possessive, even installing a listening device in the bungalow, with which he learned of Symonds' plans to dump him for another man and blackmail him on the way out. So he killed her. (BBC News 2016)

Was her radar jammed? Yes! This man had charmed her with gifts and a lavish lifestyle. He paid her to stop seeing other men, an action that could easily be mistaken for protectiveness but was more typical of fake protectiveness. They had an immediate, intense spark that tricked them into thinking they were in love. Within days their relationship turned sexual.

Jodi Arias and Travis Alexander

The relationship between Jodi Arias and Travis Alexander began with a rush of intensity. The pair met at a work convention in 2006 and hit it off immediately. Arias broke up with her live-in, long-term boyfriend later that week. She then met Alexander for a weekend stay at a friend's home in California, where they first became intimate, setting off an erotic sexual relationship.

"He said, 'I'll come into your room when they're asleep'," Arias recounted. "There was no conversation. I thought there was going to be, but there wasn't," she said. "We sat down and started passionately kissing." (Curry 2013)

The two had an instant connection and spoke on the phone every day. Court records indicate that the couple exchanged 82,000 emails (Lohr 2012). They dated for a year and then broke up, but continued to sleep together until Arias killed Alexander in a violent rage a year later. She stood trial for the murder and was sentenced to natural life in prison with no chance for release.

If you've seen Jodi Arias in the news, do you think she seems to have all of the four characteristics of an HCP? This was another example of a spark and a fast sexual connection. We don't know if she also swept him off his feet with charm, protectiveness, or fake compatibility, but her potential for violent rages was probably kept out of sight for a long time—until it killed him. Perhaps great sex was the primary way she jammed his radar—from beginning to end. As you now know, intense sexuality can sometimes cover up a high-conflict personality.

Conclusion

Our culture romanticizes the notion of a blind, headlong rush into love, one in which we follow our hearts and trust in destiny. We're proposing a new culture that approaches relationships with eyes wide open, one that isn't driven by love blindness, sexual blindness, or any other type of blindness.

Don't let your dating radar be jammed by lack of awareness. Maintain a healthy skepticism by knowing that some people, with or without good intentions, present a false exterior. They're on their best behavior—until you commit. Watch for the four most common extreme qualities: extreme charm, extreme compatibility, extreme sexuality or sensuality, and extreme protectiveness. These can be turned on high by HCPs, and then turned off once the relationship solidifies.

Do your research, talk to friends and family, and pay attention to your gut feelings if something seems amiss. Lastly, take your time. Despite looking really good for several months, within approximately a year most HCPs have shown their full range of behavior.

Of course, seeing this full range of behavior means that you can't have too many blind spots. Let's look now at how and why you can miss some of the most important warning signs.

CHAPTER THREE

What Are Your Blind Spots?

People who end up in relationships with HCPs aren't stupid. They just don't see what they need to see when they need to see it. Some are average, regular people going through life looking for love. Some are vulnerable, lonely, naïve, or desperate. The common thread is that they don't have dating radar—or if they do, they're not using it at all, they're using only part of it, they're letting it get jammed, or they're intentionally ignoring it. One way or another, there's something that makes them blind.

Again, we'd like to emphasize that it's not about intelligence. These blind spots are lapses in judgment or discernment that any of us can have. But if you know you have blind spots, and you know where they are, you can compensate for them, just as you would before changing lanes on the freeway. It's not enough to glance at the side mirror; you need to lean forward in the driver's seat to get a better look in the mirror *and* turn to look over your shoulder. This chapter is all about how to check your relationship blind spots so you don't get sideswiped.

Know Your Vulnerabilities

We can put most of our blind spots into three general categories:

1. Low self-esteem

2. Loneliness or grieving

3. Naïve beliefs

Let's take a closer look at each.

Low Self-Esteem

Low self-esteem is the belief that you don't have much worth or value as a human being. It comes primarily from life experience. If you were abused as a child, you may have concluded from experience that you're less important than other people or that it's normal for you to be treated badly. Child abuse trains us to be in a one-down position and to allow others to mistreat us. It can blind us to the fact that most people treat their children and fellow adults decently, and that this is how we ourselves deserve to be treated.

Bill once had a client, who we'll call Lucy, who hired Bill as her divorce attorney. When he asked how long she'd been married, she said, ""Six weeks."

Bill was very surprised. He said, "Don't you want to give it some time? See how things go? Maybe it's just a rocky start." Then he asked Lucy why she wanted to get divorced.

"He won't let me move into his house yet," she said. "Because his ex-girlfriend is dragging her feet moving out."

"Why did you wait so long?" Bill exclaimed, again surprised.

"Well, I didn't know what to expect for a while," she said.

As they talked, it became clear that her therapist had referred her to Bill because he had been a social worker before he was a lawyer, working with some clients who had been abused as children. And Lucy had a terrible abuse history.

Lucy's past had made her vulnerable to a man who treated her like dirt. Ironically, he didn't physically abuse her like her parents had when she was growing up. But he still talked down to her as if she were a lesser being—someone who deserved to be pushed around and disrespected and manipulated. This included telling her to stay away from his house until his prior girlfriend moved out, and allowing this to take weeks.

Bill met Lucy's husband when he came to the law office to sign the final divorce papers. This man was very self-confident and he didn't use a lawyer. Bill immediately found him to be extremely obnoxious—arrogant, rude, and disrespectful, while presenting himself as a superior being.

It was sad to realize that Lucy hadn't seen these warning signs right from the start. He had impressed her so much that she thought of him as a superior being, instead of considering that his sense of superiority could be a warning sign. Fortunately, she was in therapy, learning that her abuse as a child was totally undeserved, and that she could use this adult experience to help her to develop radar to screen out people with such high-conflict behavior in the future.

Low self-esteem can cause some people to compromise and sacrifice their wants and needs, making them more vulnerable to the extremes of the HCP. Consider the example offered by a survey respondent who commented, "My self-esteem was so low that once, while we were having sex, I picked up his phone when it started ringing and when I saw it was his ex-girlfriend, I handed it to him and waited to continue until he was finished talking with her."

Of course, low self-esteem can also result from a bad adult relationship, even for someone who wasn't abused as a child. Many people aren't prepared for a verbally abusive or physically violent partner, because their childhood upbringing was very loving and secure. It catches people off guard and slowly crushes their self-esteem. Some people then rebound into another bad relationship, because it helps them out of the first abusive relationship, and maybe because it's now familiar. Or they may just think that this one isn't as bad as the last one, not realizing that relationships can be wonderful.

Some people have low self-esteem because of some mistake that they made in the past. Maybe their first marriage was a disaster, or they made bad choices about sex, drugs, or friends. These mistakes may have led to addiction, incarceration, serious health issues, or financial problems—resulting in low self-esteem. Yet everyone makes mistakes. Some people say that everyone makes mistakes 15 percent of the time. The only difference among us is how we look at the 15 percent—in other words, how we judge ourselves or others.

If you have a blind spot caused by low self-esteem, how do you overcome it? Generally, by getting some counseling and also finding a good, supportive community of friends to help boost your self-esteem. Some find faith to be a needed component in building self-esteem.

But no one can *give* us self-esteem. We experience it by having successful relationships and doing the things that are important to us and that we enjoy doing—with others who treat us with respect and enjoyment in return.

Here's some advice from survey respondents who now understand the importance of self-esteem:

Educate yourself on high-conflict personalities, and work on your own self-esteem before seeking a partner.

Take time to really get to know the person; know who you are and how you want to be treated. You deserve the best! Don't forget to look for red flags!!!

Be realistic. Determine from the beginning what you are willing to compromise on and what issues are important and unconditional.

Loneliness or Grieving

Truth be told, most people are lonely without a partner. We're wired for relationships and lonely without them. John Cacioppo, director of the University of Chicago's Center for Cognitive and Social Neuroscience, and author of *Loneliness: Human Nature and the Need for Social Connection* (W. W. Norton & Co., 2009) has studied how loneliness affects the mind and body. Here's what he had to say in an interview about loneliness and the brain: "Humans don't do well if they're alone. If they got ostracized from the group, they were likely to perish…Loneliness is not designed to be chronic; instead, it's very much like physical pain or hunger. It's an aversive cue that alerts you to pay attention." (Entis 2016)

Interesting. We're meant to be connected to other humans and when we're not, our brains instinctively go into self-preservation mode just to survive. The brain tells us to pay attention: *Hey, you're lonely, you feel isolated, this doesn't feel good! Go meet someone! Start looking on Tinder for a face you can fall in love with.*

If you don't get connected with other humans, loneliness can turn into depression. It's the discomfort of that state of mind that often motivates us to seek human relationships, especially romantic ones, without screening our partners for bad behavior.

As one survey respondent advised: "Accept that being alone is better than being abused and lonely."

Grieving is similar to loneliness and sometimes has the same causes. Any type of loss can leave you feeling very vulnerable. Grief over a breakup or the death of a loved one (such as a spouse, parent, or child) can leave one vulnerable to an HCP who reaches out with a lot of high-energy attention.

A good example of this may be Paul McCartney, the famous Beatle, who lost the love of his life when Linda McCartney died in 1998, after thirty years of marriage. According to news reports, he met Heather Mills at an awards ceremony in May 1999, and he was immediately attracted to her. There was that spark!

He called her soon afterward and the couple began dating in July. They vacationed in New York and Long Island and by September 1999 were "spending five nights a week together."

McCartney reportedly was still grieving for Linda when he met Mills, a dynamic public figure who had lost a leg in a motorcycle accident and did a lot of high-profile charity work. A perfect partner for him, right?

They were married for six years, 2002 to 2008. It's unclear whether they lived together between 2000 and 2002, as she said they did and he said they didn't. (The court said they didn't.) Apparently, she could be very dramatic and emotional, and eventually she became too much for McCartney.

In their divorce court hearings, Mills claimed that she served as a "psychologist" to McCartney, helping him get over Linda. And she apparently made other dramatic claims. However, the family court judge said:

> "I wholly reject her account that she rekindled the husband's professional flame and gave him back his confidence. I have to say that the wife's evidence that in some way she was the husband's 'psychologist,' even allowing for hyperbole, is typical of her make-belief." (Gammell and Rayner 2008)

Bill saw Heather Mills on the news around that time (2008) and was struck by how dramatic and publicly disparaging and blaming of McCartney she appeared to be. He immediately wondered if she was an HCP, even before the judge made his findings about her "make-belief." Drama and make-believe stories often fit with histrionic personalities.

Unfortunately, we'll never know how their dating relationship actually developed, but it seems clear that he was still grieving when they met and may have had blind spots in his attraction to her. But she also may have jammed his dating radar with her good looks, exciting personality, and good works for charity. Apparently she was too good to be true.

Naïve Beliefs

The third major category of vulnerability is naïve beliefs. These typically come in three flavors:

1. Mistaking warning signs for love
2. Believing time and love will change the person
3. Believing you can change the person

Any of these beliefs can function as a blind spot. Many, if not most, people growing up in our culture carry these beliefs, which means we are set up for sticking with HCPs, even when we see some red flags. Remember, falling for an HCP doesn't mean that we're stupid. To a significant extent, it's because of our cultural conditioning. And our modern culture includes a lot of popular music, movies, TV, and the Internet.

With the advent of reality television shows, we're given a front row seat to the matchmaking process in general and blind love in particular. One such show called *Catfish* provides a perfect example of this. This wildly popular show produced by MTV profiles couples who met online sometime in the past but have never met in person. Eventually, one of them becomes suspicious about the true identity of their online love interest—usually because of a refusal to video chat or meet in person. The suspicious one reaches out to the show to find out whether the "love of their life," who they may have spent years chatting with online, is actually the person they say they are. About nine-and-a-half times out of ten they aren't.

They've been "catfished,"—a term that has evolved from this modern-day phenomenon. The show was inspired by the host's own experience of being duped by an online girlfriend and left heartbroken. The host, a young man named Nev Schulman, made a documentary (also called *Catfish*) about his experience, and it received an enormous response from others who had had similar experiences. The film was so popular that MTV created the reality series, which has introduced society to a new paradigm in dating and relationships.

Watch a few episodes and you start to see patterns of vulnerability in "catfishees." They're lonely, isolated, or shy, or they've been burned in previous relationships—just as we've been describing in this chapter.

One episode, a classic from 2016, provides a perfect example of our vulnerabilities to HCPs. A beautiful twentysomething single mother of two contacted the show's producers seeking their help to find out if the man she'd fallen in love with, after meeting him through the online dating site Tinder, was actually who he said he was. An extraordinarily beautiful woman, she'd previously posed for *Playboy* and was employed as a dancer in the entertainment industry. This was a woman who wouldn't have a hard time meeting men.

When they initially met online, she'd thought to herself

that he was extraordinarily good-looking. She commented: "Oh my gosh, you're so pretty! Here I am, a single mother of two. There's no way you're gonna want to talk to me, but I said, *Ah, give it a try.*"

Her heart and mind instantly felt attraction to this handsome guy. She spent the next six months talking to him on the phone, falling madly in love, but she never met him in person, nor had they video chatted. She'd wanted their first in-person meeting to be the first time they laid eyes on each other.

When asked what the attraction was, she said, "…we just really emotionally connected."

They talked on the phone one to two hours every day. He seemed *extremely compatible* with her. (Sound familiar?) He was supportive of everything she was about and he was accepting of her kids. It wasn't long before he asked for exclusivity in their relationship.

Over time, her friends grew more and more suspicions of her invisible knight in shining armor. Knowing she hadn't done any background checks on him, a few of her good friends took it upon themselves to do some digging and didn't like what they discovered. Things just didn't add up. So she submitted her story to the *Catfish* show to finally discover what was up with this guy.

When she contacted the show's producers, she said "I want to meet him [Lucas] face to face so I can ask why he's doing this [lying]." She explained to them that Lucas had told her he would be moving in January to Portland, Oregon, where she lived. But January came and went and she heard nothing from him.

Once the *Catfish* guys, Nev and Max, started on the case, it didn't take their producers long to find several other women in different parts of the country with alarmingly similar stories. It was the same guy—Lucas. So off they went, Nev and Max and three Lucas catfishees, to confront the catfish right in his home.

Before they arrived, one of the women explained that he'd already confessed that he wasn't who he said he was (once she pressured him to prove who he was, after she'd purchased a plane ticket to visit him). He'd confessed, "I'm not who I say I am. I'm not the guy in the pictures."

Upon arrival, the guy who answered the door indeed wasn't the handsome "Lucas" from his pictures. Not even close.

He immediately confessed that his name wasn't Lucas—it was Zac. With no hesitation, he admitted that the three women standing in his front yard were the women he'd had online and texting relationships with.

With some prompting, he stammered, "… you guys knew me as Lucas. I'm Zac. That's my real name. This all started just over a year ago. I was curious about someone who was as attractive as Lucas, the kind of reception they'd get on Tinder versus Zac, myself. I started to really enjoy the attention I was getting from people I'd never gotten attention from before. I was really happy about that. And that's where it started."

He admitted he'd "selfishly" catfished ("conned") more than 400 women. Watching and listening to this overweight, slightly nerdy-looking guy, one could almost feel a little sorry for him and understand why he started down this path.

Asked how someone like this could convince so many women that he was real, one of the women explained:

"I don't have a problem meeting guys. Being a mom was a problem. Being a dancer is a problem. It made me feel like those were things I couldn't share with anybody else, so when I made the Tinder [account], I sort of left all that stuff because I wanted somebody to get to know me and what I have to offer instead of judging me right away. Lucas made everything a little bit easier. The kid thing didn't bother him. He'd worked in a day care before."

"When I send you a personal picture, it's because I trust you."

She thought she was using her radar, and she was, but she needed yet another layer of radar—the kind that would have protected her.

The other women added bits and pieces of their stories:

"He sent me a video on Snapchat [to prove he was who he claimed he was]. It was just video of him walking out of a building and you can see his face clearly. I didn't know you could do anything on Snapchat like that. That was pretty convincing to me. That was convincing enough."

"He was kind, loving."

"He seemed like a really sweet guy."

"We talk constantly."

"He wanted to move to Wisconsin to be with me."

Regrettably for the women, they'd been sexually intimate with him both over the phone and through sexually explicit pictures they'd shared with him. (He denied still having the pictures, but his phone files proved differently.) They felt violated, and some were downright furious, devastated, or heartbroken—their trust in men further diminished, and their self-esteem swirling down the drain.

This man had set out to jam their radar and it worked—because their blind spots allowed it to happen.

Fast forward several seasons on *Catfish*, when the show

produced a few episodes in which the hosts update the audience about past episodes. In the most shocking update, the host, Nev, confessed that he'd been catfished a second time! Here's what he said about getting hooked a second time:

> "I felt like I could trust her. We had talked on the phone for a couple of months."

> "As much as I like to think I'm an expert at avoiding this type of thing, I guess I am still a dopey vulnerable romantic. Who doesn't like getting flirted with?"

Nev's current girlfriend commented:

> "I think in the world there are hopefuls and there are catfish. Nev is a hopeful and I think that's a beautiful thing."

Mistaking Warning Signs for Love

Music, movies, and TV dramas teach us to regard certain dating behaviors as expressions of devotion. But these same tendencies are actually harmful in the hands of HCPs. Extreme behavior—like constant texting or showing up uninvited, or even stalking—can be misinterpreted as signs of love. With some people these behaviors may last a day or two and never occur again. And maybe that *is* love. But with HCPs, these are warning signs of a *pattern* of *extreme behavior* (an HCP characteristic), especially when they repeat and increase over the course of the relationship. What once seemed rather cute becomes a pattern of power and control that is hard to escape.

Here are some examples from our survey:

I mistook her stalking tendencies for an expression of what I thought was her undying love for me.

One night he drove to my house (three hours away) and left gifts in my car. He shared very personal (and, I found out later, untrue) information about himself very early.

Many phone calls a day (a dozen or more). Controlling and "needing" to always be there.

Experienced very high highs—quite manic in his excitement to be with me.

Unreasonable jealousy.

Jealous love can seem endearing at the start. But many men and women have described to us how their dating partners quickly became *extremely* possessive and jealous in a way that seemed to be about power and control. Jealousy is a very common pattern with HCPs, because they feel so insecure all the time. But ongoing jealousy often turns into a power play that is very unhealthy.

Likewise, anger can be mistaken for love—as in, *Someone who cares enough to be really angry with me must be someone really committed to me.* Don't be fooled! Anger and commitment are two separate things. A pattern of anger or extreme anger is a sign of trouble, not love.

Obsessive control is another problem. Several men and women have told us about their dating partners or spouses showing up at their workplaces to find out who they are talking to and whether they are paying too much attention to people of the opposite sex on the job. The last person quoted above went on to say that her partner tried to make her feel guilty by sulking or ignoring her, or by saying things like "Why would you want to be spending time with that person?" She told us, "He didn't believe that people of the opposite gender can be just friends, even though he has social relationships with any number of female colleagues."

Believing Time and Love Will Change the Person

Many of our survey respondents said that they stayed with their dating partner *despite seeing warning signs*, because they believed that time and love would make things better. This is wishful thinking! But it's very common, especially after you get further into the relationship and it becomes harder to break up.

Here are some of the survey responses we received about this particular vulnerability. We asked:

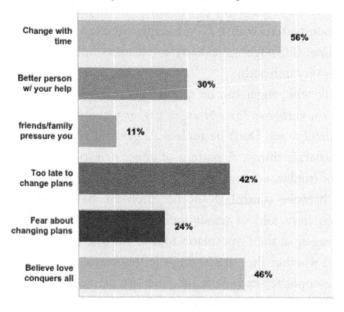

Q17 If you saw red flags, but proceeded to marry or move in, did you:

- Change with time — 56%
- Better person w/ your help — 30%
- friends/family pressure you — 11%
- Too late to change plans — 42%
- Fear about changing plans — 24%
- Believe love conquers all — 46%

More than half thought their partner would change into a better person given time, and slightly less than half believed that love would conquer all their partner's foibles. Over 40 percent said they felt it was too late to stop the wedding or change the plans, and a full third believed they could help change their partner into a better person.

Some HCPs seem to be aware of this naïve belief and will even use it to jam their partners' radar. One of our survey respondents wrote:

> *He often talked about how special my love was, that my love was saving him. He claimed that my love would help him be a better person and that no one else ever had or ever would love him the way I loved him. I fell for it hook, line, and sinker.*

The mistaken belief that people with high-conflict behavior patterns will eventually change is one of the biggest problems we have seen. This hopefulness seems nearly universal. We suspect that people feel it because they have reached a point of no return, so that it would feel too hard to reverse course and get out. They then adjust their beliefs to match the situation, rather than changing their circumstances in response to what they know is true.

Part of this developing fantasy may be that their partner will eventually "wake up and smell the coffee." That they will "get it" that their behavior is inappropriate and self-defeating. They will realize that they might lose their partner and therefore change into a loving, reasonable person.

Our rational mind wants to believe that nearly everyone is made the same way and has the same capability to change. But self-improvement requires insight, exactly what HCPs are lacking. Unfortunately, we get trapped in the mistaken belief that our love, patience, and suffering will give them insight.

The comedian Dave Chapelle once performed a comedy sketch called "The Black White Supremacist" (2003). The main character, Clayton Bigsby, was born blind and raised in a home for the blind in the Deep South. Eventually, he grew up and moved on to become an author of several racist books and a leading member of the Ku Klux Klan (a secret society of white supremacists). Never having been told that he's black, he's spent his entire life raging against African Americans. Finally the day comes when he's asked to give a talk about his book to a group of other white supremacists who look to him as a hero. While he's speaking to the crowd with his KKK robe and hood on (complete with gloves), an audience member asks him to remove his hood so they can see the face of this man they adore. You can only imagine the shock that rippled through the audience that day when they saw a black man standing before them. Their hero had been black all along. Up to that moment, he'd operated as a white man. He'd never had insight into the reality of his skin color.

There are many parallels between HCPs and Mr. Bigsby, including lack of insight about a characteristic that isn't going to change. But Mr. Bigsby finally found out he wasn't white, whereas HCPs, in general, do not have the same revelation about their HCP status.

This is perhaps the most important point we want to make with this book, so it bears repeating:

High-conflict people have a narrow range of negative behavior that they repeat and repeat without changing, for their entire lives, even when it is self-defeating.

This point remains true, regardless of the amount of time and love that you put into your relationships with them. We must *acknowledge* and *accept* that they have a high-conflict personality, and have our radar up to watch for this problem in the first place.

Believing You Can Change the Person

Many survey respondents told of getting hooked into a sense of responsibility for an HCP dating partner, or a fantasy that they could change the person. Here's what some of them said:

> Don't ever think you can change anyone. Either accept everything about them or leave them.

> Do not think you can change someone, because you can't. They have to want to change, and narcissists won't. It's all about them.

HCPs often see romantic love as unequal: one person should be responsible for the other person. This explains the "protective" quality that many people notice in the early stage of the relationship. An HCP may "need" to be protective, or they may "need" you to be protective of them. Either way, this is a trap. Their needs will never end.

While it feels good to hear that we have a powerful, positive impact on the other person, it can soon become exhausting with HCPs because their neediness or drive to dominate takes over.

This dynamic is different from healthy relationships that involve one partner caring for the other who has an illness or disability or other burden. In these relationships, the situation is straightforward and clear-cut, with limits to the caretaking, and the relationship has other characteristics that make it balanced and equal. There is a mutuality to it; you may be doing most of the caretaking right now, but they truly would take care of you if and when you needed it. With HCPs, it is a manipulation that draws you in and then reveals itself to be a bottomless pit. The fantasy is that you will be able to change the person, rescue them from their problems, and then the neediness or drive for power and control will come to an end. But it's just that—a fantasy. So forget about it!

Address Your Vulnerabilities as Blind Spots

The more vulnerable you are, the more blind you may be in dating. Some of these vulnerabilities are best addressed in counseling, especially when they arise from a history of child abuse, long-standing loneliness, or prolonged grieving of a lost relationship.

The other vulnerabilities are naïve beliefs. If those are in play, you'll need to train yourself not to misinterpret warning signs, such as obsessive jealousy, stalking, constant contact, showing up by surprise, and so forth. Having a good support system and asking friends for feedback can help a lot with this.

Likewise, reminding yourself (and having others remind you) of this basic reality can be helpful:

Time and love will not change a high-conflict person for the better. *You* cannot change a high-conflict person for the better.

Depending on your life experience and the messages you received growing up, these vulnerabilities can create larger or smaller blind spots. They can be the biggest factor setting you up to miss all the warning signs available to your radar, if you let them. Don't let them! Make the effort to become aware of your potential blind spots, and be sure to check them carefully before you change lanes.

Putting It All Together

At this point, you've learned:

1. Warning signs of certain personalities that can spell relationship danger

2. Ways they can jam your radar (deceive you)

3. Where your own blind spots might be

Now, let's hone your dating radar by looking at how these three things fit together.

Most people don't know the warning signs of the predictable patterns of high-conflict people. (You've learned some of these patterns in previous chapters, and we'll go into these patterns in more depth in the next four chapters.) Add to that, HCPs can jam your radar with the extreme qualities of attraction (charm, apparent compatibility, sex, and protectiveness). The effects of chemistry and attraction are powerful, almost irresistible forces that seem to give you the green light to proceed. They tell you this person is "the one" to spend your life with.

Add the alleviation of loneliness and grieving and it feels even more right. Add sex (if you haven't already). Add some naïve beliefs about people changing their extremely bad behavior, and you have the trifecta of perfect relationship nirvana, a recipe for happily ever after. Except, as you now know, it's actually a recipe for disaster.

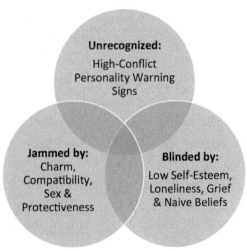

As we mentioned before, this extreme combination of three types of radar dysfunction can be covered up by incredibly wonderful feelings. Remember the chemicals: dopamine, oxytocin, and endorphins. Dopamine gets us excited (especially sexually) about our partner, while oxytocin increases feelings of warmth, love, attachment, and trust. Endorphins contribute to a "peaceful, euphoric bliss." (Doidge 2007)

Our brains love being in love. But overall these chemicals can cloud our thinking and skew our memories so that we view things as much rosier than they really are. There's nothing wrong with having these wonderful feelings, so long as you also use your dating radar before you commit.

Think back to the story of the millionaire and the escort in chapter 2. She (and possibly he) was probably not thinking about using dating radar to identify high-conflict personality warning signs, of which there were many. It's also likely that her radar was jammed by his charm and protectiveness, and the sex that began early in the relationship. Her blind spots may have included low self-esteem, loneliness as a single mom, and grief over the loss of a past boyfriend. In her case, the combination of these radar dysfunctions turned out to be deadly.

As for the case of Travis Alexander and Jodi Arias, we can only speculate on what he thought and felt about her. He did split up with her after about a year, which was a year before she killed him. Perhaps he was temporarily blinded by sex and intense emotions, and then his mind cleared enough to realize she had some high-conflict traits. She obviously was a very disturbed person. Yet he apparently had no clue how dangerous she could become, during or after the relationship. One lesson from this story: it's far better to avoid getting into this type of relationship than to try to remove yourself after an HCP has formed a deep attachment to you. Blind spots can be dangerous.

Only rarely do high-conflict relationships end fatally; however, do you think either of these people who ultimately lost their lives had an inkling their lives would be taken from them by the person who professed to love them most?

The majority of high-conflict relationships are not deadly. Nonetheless, they can be extremely harmful physically, mentally, and emotionally.

How Would Life Be Different with Better Dating Radar?

Now that you know how your radar can be jammed, and how your blind spots can set you up for dating a high-conflict person, think about how your choices might be different if you had reliable dating radar.

In our survey, we asked whether respondents would have entered into a relationship with the high-conflict person if they'd known the difficulties ahead. Nearly three-fourths of survey respondents said they would *not* have entered into the relationship. Only 9 percent would have entered it, and 17 percent were unsure.

Of those who said *unsure* or *yes*, most gave qualified answers like these:

The only reason I would is because I have a wonderful son from the relationship. If I had not had a child then I definitely would not.

This may be different than most answers. This person had a daughter, and while she was not the reason that I entered the relationship, she is the reason that I stayed and that I would not do it any differently. I cannot imagine my life without her as my

Q12 Would you have entered into a relationship with this person if you'd known the difficulties ahead?

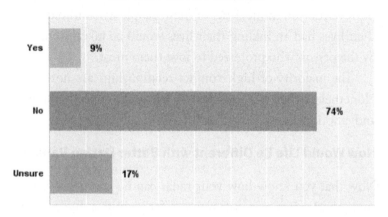

daughter regardless of how much pain was endured to make it so. With respect to the person, I realize now that I did not—nor do I now—have the skills to help her. I still hope that she gets the help needed.

Had I not, I would not have my son, but I fear sometimes, because he is a lot like his dad: charming and manipulative, hot-tempered, physically aggressive, etc.

Here's what some of those who said *no* had to say:

Hindsight is almost always 20/20. At times I wish I had left earlier. I tolerated far more than I should have for way too many years.

Came to the realization that having grown up in an alcoholic family I had a codependent personality. I was going to fix her.

Oh, hell no! It's like dating somebody who has crazy mood swings, vacillates between nice and nasty, inconsistent stories, like they are a tornado or torturing you at times. It's absolutely exhausting. They say something and then when you confront them on it they act like they never said it or say you got the story wrong. They blame or try to shame you for something that they actually do.

I thought that with time and love I could help him to feel more secure and confident and be happier. I was wrong. There were times when it looked like I was succeeding but ultimately things were getting worse.

My life would have been completely different without him in it. Instead, my life is shattered and I am only a small fraction of the person I used to be. My physical health is ruined. My mental health is destroyed. I have lost all the joy and hope that I used to have. He has also ruined my kids' lives, causing my youngest to be suicidal, and my oldest is a ticking time bomb.

Honestly, it took me a while to break a pattern of relationships with men just like this. I was aware of the pattern before I entered the relationship, but I hoped that the relationship was different and I had met someone different. I soon realized that I was repeating the same pattern, though. I was learning slowly. Over a course of five to ten years I did a lot of work on myself, eventually breaking the pattern, and met a stable, loving man who I am in a committed relationship with now.

It's sobering, isn't it? We share these comments to help you understand the end result of relationships with HCPs. It's not pretty. Some tough it out, finding a way to protect themselves while remaining in the relationship. Others do it for the sake of the kids or because they're not in a financial position to leave. Some stay because their self-worth is so low they're willing to accept bread crumbs. But the majority wish they'd never made a commitment to an HCP.

Most of us avoid dating the obvious "bad" guys, like criminals and terrorists, but like we said before, HCPs don't come with a neon "HCP" sign or an HCP tattoo on their foreheads. (Wouldn't it be nice if they did?) So it's easy to miss the signs, especially if we're not looking for them, or they jam our radar, or we're vulnerable in some way.

Even if you're aware of some red flags, like obvious lying or refusal to introduce you to family, there may be many other warning signs that are less obvious, and some of them can even be mistaken for proof that this person is "the one."

The trouble is in not understanding that some people are truly relationship destroyers and some can even be fatally dangerous. Not only is there a gap in societal awareness, there's a widespread refusal to accept the reality that some people simply are not capable of being part of a healthy relationship and will, in fact, make your life miserable, destroy your trust in humanity, harm you, alienate your children against you, divide your family, decimate your career, drain your bank account, land you in jail, or, in the worst cases, kill you. It's probably fair to say that most people in relationships with HCPs are completely unaware that their partners are walking time bombs.

If you're not using radar, or your radar is jammed, or you have big blind spots, you are a prime target. The HCPs force field is strong, and they will mislead you, at least temporarily. It may seem harsh to brand a group of people in such a negative light, but allow us to explain: Their relationship operating system is driving them to do whatever it takes to keep the anxiety monster away. This operating system dictates that they have to attach to you, dominate you, be superior to you, or be the center of attention.

Strangely enough, they don't even know they're doing this, even while they are. What this means at the beginning is that they're compelled to put their best self in front of you when they meet you. So naturally, they'll manipulate you.

But you should know that the conning is not intentional for all of them—even though, when you're in a high-conflict relationship, it can feel as if it is entirely intentional. Some of the true HCP con artists, like antisocial (sociopath) HCPs, do seek out vulnerable people. Other HCPs, like borderlines, are simply miserable without romantic connection (and sadly, many are miserable with it, too). Remember, it's tricky, so that's why you have to be aware. You have to know yourself and always have your radar on when you're looking for love—and especially before you sign on the dotted line.

Conclusion

The very qualities that help us fall in love can at the same time be the on-ramp for the highway to hell. Avoiding a high-conflict relationship requires looking beyond attraction, chemistry, availability, and compatibility, and recognizing your own particular blind spots.

Three types of fact-finding are essential:

1. Looking for warning signs of certain personalities that can spell relationship danger
2. Recognizing the ways that HCPs can jam your radar (deceive you)
3. Knowing where your own blind spots might be

Now that your eyes are wide open to how HCPs can jam your radar, and you understand how your own vulnerabilities can blind you, let's take a closer look at the four different high-conflict personalities.

CHAPTER FOUR

Don't Kiss a Narcissist!
"You show up for them; they don't show up for you."

Core Fear – Being Inferior

Chances are that you *will* kiss a narcissist someday, if you haven't already. According to a major study done by the National Institutes of Health (NIH), slightly over 6 percent of the United States adult population meets the criteria for narcissistic personality disorder (Stinson et al. 2008). Many more may have milder narcissistic traits, but not the disorder.

So you will meet narcissists for sure. The trick is to spot them on your radar.

In this chapter, we'll talk about narcissistic HCPs' classic pattern of dating and relationship behavior. Then we'll explain their special ways of jamming your radar. Finally, we'll address common blind spots—the vulnerabilities you might have that set you up to fall for a narcissist.

Narcissists are the most common type of HCP. They can make your life truly miserable because of their drive to pick targets of blame and then, well, *blame them*—for everything. So you'll want to be sure your dating radar is super sharp when it comes to these folks. Keep in mind that not all narcissists are HCPs—some are just self-absorbed and don't necessarily blame others.

Fear Factor: Inferiority

The narcissistic HCP is driven by a *fear that they are inferior*. Underneath it all, they have gigantic feelings of shame and worthlessness. They are unconsciously terrified that other people will see them as weak, useless, or unimportant. Under the influence of this emotional cocktail, they have no possible reaction other than to try to relieve these feelings of shame by *showing that they are superior*, all of the time. They are constantly seeking power, control, and status. (Remember, don't try to point this out to them. They will only react with anger for weeks, months or years.)

Narcissist HCP
FEAR OF BEING **INFERIOR**
Demanding Demeaning Self-absorbed Insulting
Needs to be **superior**

What makes a narcissist feel inferior?

- Anything that makes them feel one-upped
- Your success
- Your bigger home or more expensive car
- Trips you've taken
- Relationships with other people
- Important people you know
- Events you're hosting or attending
- Stories you tell
- Experiences you've had
- Your paying attention to someone else
- Their perception of being disrespected
- Anything that carries a whiff of failure
- Anything that provokes even a momentary a sense of self-doubt
- Being called or being perceived as a loser

The instant any of these feelings of inferiority are triggered—whether by their own internal fears or by external events—they must knock someone down a peg by insulting, demeaning, mocking, or controlling them. This kind of reaction is truly involuntary for narcissistic HCPs. They're programmed this way, although they don't know it. And you may be the target, even if the feeling of inferiority was triggered by someone else.

Narcissistic HCPs have a built-in "Spidey sense" that is constantly gathering and assessing information about threats to its superiority. They have to destroy the threat before it destroys them. They don't think before pulling the trigger and firing off an insult or put-down. They shoot first and never question themselves later. They immediately feel justified in their action because their anxiety begins to calm once the feeling of superiority fills them once again. The fact that the behavior makes them feel better convinces them that they were right.

Meanwhile, you've been insulted and want to explain, argue, shut down, or run from the conversation. You're emotionally hooked. You know you've been drawn in if you find yourself explaining your actions, justifying yourself, blowing up, running from the room, or using physical force like pushing, hitting, or shoving. And when you get hooked, they win.

Here are two sad stories to illustrate how hurtful narcissistic HCPs can be—and how they can catch you by surprise.

The Gold Digger

"I was surprised when Brandi, an ex-girlfriend of one of my good friends, wanted to hook up with me. After their relationship ended, he never discussed it. We were both typical nerdy forty-year-old tech guys who owned our own successful software

companies. She was an attractive blonde in her thirties, very charming. She seemed to know everyone who was important in town and claimed to be well connected to executives in the country's giant tech firms. She was quite the name-dropper. She was a college professor and an excellent conversationalist, able to draw just about anyone into conversation.

She seemed like the complete package, so I went for it. I fell for her almost immediately. We had a great time at first, and the only thing that made me uncomfortable was that it seemed like she was only happy if I was spending money on her. And although she wanted me to pick where we would go and what we would do on dates, she almost always axed my suggestions, saying she wanted a more expensive restaurant, better seats—anything that ended up costing me more. If I bought my sister or mom a present, she wanted a more expensive present.

Looking back, I still can't believe I was so naïve. I bought a car I couldn't afford, using money meant to invest in my business, to take it to the next stage of growth. I thought she'd love the car and be impressed, but no, she said I was stupid for buying it. She demanded the very best clothes, jewelry, trips, and restaurants.

She told me I didn't make enough money for her and that I'd led her to believe that I had more money. Mind you, I make a very good living and spent most of it on her, but it was never enough. She wanted more, better, bigger. I put my finances and my business in jeopardy for her. I tolerated the put-downs, the attacks on my ability to provide for her. Over the year we dated, I became a shadow of my former self but didn't see it at the time. I felt incompetent, impotent.

The list of horrible things she did to me was endless. Arriving home from work, I'd find my pillow on the doorstep, meaning

I was relegated to my car for the night. She called me names like "idiot," "stupid," "f——ing a—hole." Told me she hated me. I never raised my voice or my hand to her—not once.

I deluded myself into staying with her, even asking her to marry me. She said she wanted to marry me, and we even set a date, but she suddenly dropped me. She woke me up one Saturday morning and said, "I love you so much. You are so wonderful. But I'm going to be traveling for work the next couple of weeks and I'll be mostly out of touch. I'll call you when I can." She never did.

Circling back to my friend who'd also dated her, we compared stories. They were almost identical.

Let's break it down. This poor chap was next on Brandi's target list. She was seeking someone to whom she could feel superior, someone she could put down without risk of retaliation. She picked a guy with money and no girlfriend to compete with. She wanted more of everything—material things, that is—so he gave more and more and watched his bank account balance dwindle. He allowed her to put him down, mock him, call him names.

Where was his vulnerability? He saw himself as a nerdy tech guy who couldn't "get the girl"—the kind of girl that football players get. He sacrificed his wants and needs, allowing himself to nearly go broke financially and emotionally. What was left? No relationship. Looking back on it, though, we think she may have done him a favor by leaving.

Momma's Golden Boy

My husband and I met on a beach while on vacation in Mexico. Oddly enough, we were both from the same city back in the States. He was tall, handsome, and charming, owned his own successful business, and was in charge of his life. We hit it off immediately.

He was impressed that I held a title as a beauty pageant queen and had competed on a national level. He told me I was the most beautiful woman in the world and he was proud to show me off everywhere he went.

He made me feel special and protected. Most meaningful to me was becoming part of his family. My parents were always in conflict before (and after) they divorced, and neither of them had much to do with their own families, so I suppose I was longing to belong to a family. They were the all-American, "apple pie" kind of family. He seemed to have a special relationship with his mom. And a guy who treats his mom well will treat his wife well. Or so I thought.

After we married, I learned that his mom had worshipped him as her special "golden child." She'd set him up to be adored and treated as special by everyone. She did everything for him his whole life. She even called him her "little king." She was convinced that he was smarter, more talented, more gifted than anyone, and adamant that he should never have to struggle for anything.

My expectations of happiness, security, love, and protection were dashed soon after the wedding and even more so after our first child was born. He was jealous of the attention I paid to the baby and even more so with our second child. He wanted all the attention and all the credit for providing for us. He wanted confirmation that we would be nothing if it weren't for him.

Eventually I caught him in an affair, and then another. He was furious and blamed me for being so frigid that he had to cheat! He'd been taught that he could do no wrong.

His control and rage ballooned over time. The more I shrank, the more empowered he became. I was never allowed to question him about anything. Because I'd grown up in a broken home, I was fiercely committed to my marriage and raising our kids in a two-parent home. Divorce was not a solution. I wouldn't do that to my kids. I would suck it up and be content with feeling single and alone.

He controlled where I went, who I talked to, who and what could come in the house, who I could be friends with, just about everything. I did what he asked in order to avoid fights. I just couldn't take them.

Eventually I met a man (a married father who held status in the state where we lived) who showered me with affection, attention, and love. I fell head over heels. I knew it was wrong but even though I intended to stop it, I didn't…until we were discovered by my husband.

Then the rage, bullying, humiliation, and punishment began. He called me "whore," "slut," "bitch," and every other denigrating name in the book. He questioned me relentlessly about everything. I would no longer be allowed to sleep in our bed, go anywhere without permission, use the phone without him listening. I slept on the floor in another room. I was punished severely and threatened with exposure to his family, my place of employment, our children, and the community. And he vowed to expose the man with whom I'd had the affair to the news media.

This went on for months. I morphed into an obedient, robotic wife and complied with everything he wanted. Eventually, he agreed to go to counseling but only to a male counselor of his choosing. In the opening minutes of our first session he manage to paint himself as the victim and accuse me of everything he'd actually done. He was so believable. With tears in his eyes he explained how he'd never be able to trust me again. The grossly uninformed and misguided counselor consoled him and suggested that his trust problems could be alleviated somewhat by putting a tracking device on my car.

We remain married and I continue trying to learn how to manage him. I do it because divorcing him would expose my children to his narcissism without my counterbalancing protection. At least I'm there to limit and mitigate the damage to them. I realize I'm sacrificing my own relationship happiness, but I'm content with my choice for now. My friends think I should get divorced but I'm just not ready for that.

Let's break it down. He chose to marry someone who made him look good and then had many affairs, each forgiven by his wife. Because of her past experience, she was extremely vulnerable to his charm and protectiveness, which turned into control and isolation. She was starved for attention and affection when she met someone who filled her love tank. Then came punishment and retribution.

What's Special About Narcissists?

Narcissists have key personality traits in common, and they have their own classic pattern of behavior in "love" relationships. Let's take a look.

Key Characteristics

From our experiences and observations, narcissists typically have the following characteristics in their relationships. (Note that from now on we are talking about those with narcissistic personality disorder *and* those with just narcissistic traits.) It can be difficult to understand why narcissists would behave in these ways when doing so can actually sabotage their own goals to be seen as superior, to be highly respected, and to get lots of positive attention. Instead, people start looking down on them, seeing them as ridiculous people and deserving of insults, and choosing not to be around them. But narcissists are blind to their own behavior and the problems it creates.

1. They see the world in all-or-nothing terms, primarily as winners and losers.

2. Everyone is all good or all bad. As their romantic partner, you're on the good list—at least you are for now. You will quickly be shifted to the bad list when they feel you've stolen their spotlight.

3. They see themselves as superior people (one of the winners) and are constantly promoting themselves to others. Selling themselves to everyone around them is as natural as breathing.

4. They are constantly insulting others (the losers). The moment their inferiority button is activated, their anxiety increases and they must put you or someone down to soothe their fear.

5. They eventually put down their relationship partners. At first, you are one of the winners. When they insult a loser, they seek your agreement and want you to put down that person, too. But the time will come when you shift to the loser list, and the narcissist will put *you* down, very likely in front of others, to make themselves look good, right, in control, or smart in comparison.

6. They are completely self-absorbed. ("It's all about me. Why wouldn't it be?") They often forget about their partner's existence. A narcissistic parent loves their child but can't entirely make the child's needs a priority over their own. For example, a narcissistic parent with a child who has a medical emergency will rush the child to the hospital, but the parent's focus is on their own panic and how the emergency affects them.

7. They are terrible listeners, always steering conversations back to themselves. Your needs and thoughts aren't important; only theirs are.

8. They are easily offended and viciously attack those who they believe have disrespected them. They will do this even if the offense was minor or nonexistent. They have to, because they cannot afford to see themselves as inferior, even for a second.

9. They see partners and children either as trophies or as harmful to their image. If you make them look good, you're a trophy; if you make them look even slightly bad, you're an embarrassment to be kept hidden or demeaned in public.

10. They can become extremely verbally abusive, and some are physically abusive. The more inferior they feel, the higher the anxiety, and the more likely they are to resort to verbal or physical abuse in an attempt to regain control or superiority.

11. They "split" friends, children, coworkers, and others against each other. They are dividers, not uniters. ("Either you're with me or you're against me.")

12. They are insulted when you pay too much attention to the kids, spend time with your friends or family members ("I should be enough family for you!"), or don't give them special treatment. They may hold double standards about things like money or freedom—for instance, they are allowed to stay out late, but you're not.

13. They are constantly seeking new attention from new people, and higher status from higher-status people. The need to be seen as superior makes them social climbers.

14. They may leave you suddenly for someone else.

By now you probably get the picture. We bet you can recall running into someone like this in the past—perhaps you've even dated someone like this or been married to them. At the beginning of a romance with a narcissist, you are very likely to experience the time of your life. You may feel butterflies or be very flattered by their attention. But at the same time—or within a short time—you'll have a knot in your stomach or a nagging thought at the back of your mind that something isn't right. Don't ignore it.

We won't go into explaining all of the characteristics listed above, but we do want to say more about the last four.

Domestic Violence

Narcissists are one of the personalities we see in relationships that include hitting, shoving, punching, physically restraining, breaking your possessions, blocking you from leaving, throwing your belongings away, hiding your keys, taking away your phone, and other abusive behaviors. These are legally considered domestic violence in most jurisdictions and can be the basis for restraining orders or criminal charges. These behaviors can endanger your well-being and even your life.

Here's what two survey respondents wrote:

...violence toward me, verbal and physical, and then blamed me for provoking him.

Restrained me, verbally put me down, controlling, alienated me from my friends, sabotaged my food to avoid having a "fat wife."

Not all narcissists are violent. But all narcissistic HCPs get unreasonably angry, because the world never gives them enough credit for how wonderful they think they are, and they have to blame somebody. So expect them to become abusive—at least verbally, if not worse—once they feel secure in the relationship. One of our survey respondents explained:

He had a plausible sounding story/explanation/excuse for everything. If I or anyone else pointed out that his story did not make sense, or if we contradicted anything he told us, he would rage at us. He bulldozed us into the ground...screaming at us, demanding an apology from us for accusing him of things he didn't do, accusing us of being disloyal to him. It was like a senator filibustering.

You may feel like you're constantly being coerced to do things their way. Think "control freak." Their need to feel superior outweighs your needs and any compassion for you. In fact, observe their empathy toward you and others. Narcissistic HCPs usually lack true empathy, even though they may fake it sometimes.

In the beginning you may mistake intensity for attraction or love. But be warned: the relationship can devolve into abuse and violence.

"Splitting"

Splitting describes a dynamic associated most frequently with borderline and narcissistic personality disorders. These folks truly see people as all good or all bad. For narcissists, this means they see people as superior or inferior, with no in-between. Narcissists don't unite people unless it somehow calms their fears of feeling inferior and makes them look good. Mostly they divide. In fact, they don't feel good unless they're involved in some type of drama that splits people.

Narcissists constantly engage in splitting with their family members. They often view their own children as either superior or inferior, or sometimes one of each. They want you, as the spouse or partner, to choose between them and your parents, siblings, even children or stepchildren (especially stepchildren). Narcissists divide families.

Splitting happens at work, too, where narcissists have their "superior" colleagues and those they may publicly harass or bully for being inferior. They tend to kiss up to the administrators above them and step on those below them in the hierarchy. As bosses, they like to provoke conflict among the people who report to them.

Narcissists even split their friends. They may start rumors or badmouth one friend to another.

Here's how partners of narcissistic HCPs describe their experience:

> *Every encounter had a winner and a loser, even sharing a meal had a winner and a loser.*
>
> *We fought whenever we were going to see my family or friends.*
>
> *During our custody dispute, he would change his mind frequently,*

rage at me then try to be nice to me, and incite conflict between his family and me, or his lawyer and me.

If he met one of my friends who was not part of his fan club, he would not even greet them when they came to my house. He would walk out of the room without saying a word. Or he would say rude things to me in front of them.

Although narcissists see people as either good or bad—winners or losers, superior or inferior, with no in between—they can (and will) move people from one category to the other and back again. Today's best friend may be tomorrow's idiot in their eyes and in their words. It all depends on whether they think the person reflects well on them or has slighted them in some way.

If you are their partner, they will ask you to join them in belittling others who they see as inferior, or who they feel threatened by. Confidences are usually not secure with them. They may publicly put you on the spot by saying, "Honey, tell them what you said to me about so-and-so." If you don't join in their insults about others, they'll end up insulting *you*. See how it works? If you make them look bad, they have to make *you* look bad in order to feel better. As the partner of a narcissist, you may find yourself agreeing with them about other people (or acting as if you do) as a way to get them to calm down or get off your back—because disagreeing puts you in the doghouse.

Sooner or later, you will be on the inferior side of their split. In fact, you'll find yourself thrown under the bus again and again. However, you may get back on the okay side by buttering them up. They often don't even see that you are buttering them up, because they are so eager to hear praise and admiration. Narcissists may seem canny, but their insecurity makes them blind to even the most obvious flattery.

They often have no public restraints on what they will say. They cannot help themselves. They're driven by a fear of feeling inferior, so their operating system is programmed to stay on superior mode. The second they feel inferior, they have to do whatever it takes to feel superior again.

Narcissistic Injuries

Inside of themselves, narcissists are constantly feeling disrespected. They have to fight back against these negative feelings, anxieties, and impressions—often called "narcissistic injuries"—which they overcompensate for by attacking others and puffing up their own importance over and over again. They create problems that didn't exist. It's a never-ending process, because they have distorted perceptions of themselves and profound insecurities that they can't ever soothe.

When real life doesn't treat them as superior, special people, they can become very hurt and angry. When you pay more attention to other people (your kids, your family members, friends, and so forth), they may become very upset. When others succeed publicly, they feel threatened and get very upset. They have to put you down. They have to win. They have to make you one of the losers. Since they are wonderful, superior beings, when there's a conflict "It's all your fault!" When their imperfections are exposed, they get very upset.

Here's what our survey respondents said:

If attention was paid to me that was not rewarding for him, my husband would have "panic attacks." My good times (birthday, work promotions, anything celebrating me) always resulted in one of these attacks, which meant an immediate departure during the middle of the event. Predictably, these did not happen at his events. It was so embarrassing. I ended up having to do a lot of things alone just to avoid the feigned panic attacks, but this only resulted in anger and accusations that I was cheating on him. Once that started happening, a slow isolation journey began.

She had a "Poor me, I am hard done by" attitude. Sense of entitlement, especially around money. Inability to accept that I could have a different opinion from hers.

Had to always be the "most important person" at any family gathering. For example, on Mother's Day she was really put out by another family member who had just become a mother and who stole the limelight from her.

We were both into eating healthy and fitness, but he acted competitive with me about it, like he had to prove he knew more than I did, looked better than I did, and so on, while simultaneously telling me how great I looked. It was very confusing.

The narcissistic personality usually has its origins in childhood, but it can arise in two distinctly different ways. Some narcissists grew up with an underlying sense of shame and inadequacy. Often, but not always, this comes from an abusive childhood (from verbal abuse to physical abuse). These narcissists tend to have "hot anger" and go into a rage when they are exposed as not perfect and wonderful. You can think of them as "vulnerable narcissists" or "benign narcissists." They usually weren't parented well and might not have become narcissists if not for the bad parenting. As children, they suffer from a lack of love and nurturance. Eventually they become needy and draining on others. They really cannot tolerate feeling inferior.

Other narcissists seem to have grown up being treated

well—too well. Their parents taught them that they were special and superior to everyone else. They learned to become "entitled," expecting better treatment than others got and learning from an early age that the rules don't apply to them. These are known as "grandiose narcissists." If someone causes them a narcissistic injury, they get upset, but not in the same way. They may simmer and seek revenge later. We think of this as "cold anger," compared to the "hot anger" of the vulnerable narcissists.

This entitlement is evident in the "golden boy" example earlier in the chapter. His mother groomed him to expect superior treatment from everyone around him. Her praise, adoration, and overprotection programmed his complicated operating system into one of narcissism. She didn't do it intentionally. She truly loved her son and wanted the best for him, but she went about it the wrong way.

Seeking Higher Status

Narcissists can never really absorb a feeling of relief in their sense of superiority. They typically remain anxious, and so they push themselves to gain a stronger sense of security from others. They are relentlessly concerned with image, status, prestige, wealth, their place in the hierarchy—anything that they think reflects well on them.

...she had a preoccupation with image.

He is a know-it-all. False bravado. Always justified spending money to make himself look better but wouldn't allow me to spend money on things I wanted.

They tend to be always on the lookout for more admiration, more intensity and love from more people. It's not unusual for them to have one or two affairs going during a marriage. In their mind, it's justified. They can justify anything.

My ex had affair after affair. He was never satisfied with me or any woman after me. As soon as he met a woman with more money, a bigger house on the golf course, a large alimony settlement, or a trust fund, he was on it like a fly on s——. He never apologized. He blamed each woman for the divorce. They got so sick of him that they were glad to be rid of him and more than happy to part with some of their money to see him go.

Those who get into relationships with narcissists are often surprised at this philandering, when it was predictable to others outside the relationship. Some split up with their narcissistic partner once they discover their affairs. Others grow to tolerate it for some other benefit, such as financial security, the success of a shared business, fame by association, political image, high-status lifestyle, or holding the family together for the sake of the children (although this often doesn't last). Or they develop their own secret life.

As the partner of a narcissist, you may be a means to an end. In other words, there may be something about you—looks, status, wealth—that serves the needs of the narcissistic personality. Your connection with them is rewarding for them, but it's not mutually beneficial. And worse, it will inflict lifelong damage and destruction. Plus, they are notorious for dumping partners or spouses when someone "better" comes along.

By the Numbers

In answer to the question:

Would you consider your partner to have traits of one of the following personality disorders?

Approximately 45 percent of the survey respondents said narcissistic personality disorder. This was the largest group in our survey.

Also, 26 percent said their partner had a combination of narcissistic and borderline personality disorders. When we discuss borderline personality disorder in the next chapter, you will see that it can be a more difficult situation when someone has both of these sets of problems.

Likewise, about 17 percent said their partner had narcissistic and antisocial personality disorder. In chapter 6, you will learn about the characteristics of antisocial personality. Again, this can be a powerful combination of difficulties.

Here are a couple of survey comments that may reflect a narcissistic personality:

Big shottism, high-maintenance, overspending, when he didn't have a pot to piss in. All vain qualities in my book, and not admirable, but at least he had taste and wasn't gross…and my biggest red flag was I found myself rationalizing and covering his behaviors, versus critiquing and discussing them. I knew I didn't want to upset him. I knew he had a temper that I never wanted to see.

He was always seeking attention in the nightclub scene we hung out in. Turning heads was very important to him, and he made friends with all the popular people. He played a role of being innocent and naïve, but knew exactly what he was doing. At the time, I thought he was endearing. I fell for his act like everyone else.

Narcissists have incredible skill at making a person they once seemingly adored feel inept, hopelessly stupid, and worthless. It's such a gradual process, and an empathetic person has a hard time imagining how someone could be so malevolent.

How Narcissists Jam Your Radar

Your radar is meant to detect threats of danger. Narcissistic HCPs have sophisticated ways to saturate your radar with noise or false information that tricks you into ignoring the alerts.

CHARM

Narcissists mostly jam your radar with lots and lots of charm at the beginning. In hindsight, some describe narcissists in the beginning of the relationship as exceptionally, exceedingly charming—to an intoxicating level.

> *It was almost like an elixir or a drug that was too good to be true. It felt so great, like I was the luckiest person ever to be treated so well. Who wouldn't want that?*

Keep in mind that just as narcissists can turn on the charm, they can also turn it off again.

Their stories and dreams are big. They can give the appearance of being very popular, but there often is little substance to it. They can keep you impressed and distracted by their stories of knowing important people, being in important places, and doing incredible things in their work. They're the biggest name-droppers on the planet. In fact, they lead with who they know, who they're friends with, where they've been, vacations they've taken, exotic locations they've visited, positions they hold or have held, and endless stories about themselves. If you think it's a one-time report, pay attention to see if it's a pattern. It usually is.

They are dedicated to creating a false image that is extremely superior, successful, wealthy, well connected, and so forth. Mental health professionals have called this the "false self" of narcissists. It's a defense mechanism against how vulnerable and ashamed they may feel at their core. They can't be in touch with that part because it's too painful. In fact, if they had to be exposed to this part of themselves, they might have a traumatic breakdown. They truly can't look there. So they create this false image, try to believe in it themselves, and try to get you to believe in it too.

They may even publish a book about themselves that glorifies everything about them. They truly cannot see that it's not important to anyone else, or that it's just normal life and no one really cares.

He was moderately successful in his career but always made it seem more impressive than it was.

It's all about me. It has to be. Otherwise, the inferior feeling causes anxiety. It's so predictable. It has to be all about them nearly 100 percent of the time.

Some narcissistic HCPs are all about blatant self-promotion, but with others the strategy is a faked humility. They seem to hold back, but if you listen closely, you'll notice that they pepper conversations with who they know, what they've done, what they've done, and where they've been. They may appear humble, but even that for a narcissist is an *all about me* move. In reality, humility is a manipulative act meant to make them look even better.

Typically, narcissistic HCPs like to show off and look great to everyone else. This characteristic is typical and can be so intense that you start to believe it. These are some of the people who really seem too good to be true. It can be hard to check out their stories, and they often want you to believe them on faith.

Sometimes they will tell you sad stories of how awfully

people have treated them. This is a surprising and distracting tactic. If they are so wonderful, then why do people treat them so unfairly? But this is a common aspect of this personality: bragging, combined with whining about poor treatment.

Occasionally, narcissists may be more rule-bound and moralistic. Uptight and contained. This kind may be less likely to focus on targets of blame.

Overt Sexuality

Narcissists often fake compatibility, but just temporarily as part of their initial seduction pattern. They certainly are sexually driven. Early in the relationship, this can translate into being very seductive, paying extreme attention to you, and doing everything they can to seem appealing to you. All the while they are jamming your radar with a flurry of activity focused on you. But once they achieve their seduction, their interest starts to drift elsewhere. This seduction may be starting a sexual relationship as quickly as possible, or "landing you" for a long-term commitment as their partner to show off to the public.

The overt sexuality is part of their tendency to have multiple affairs, even when they're married. This need to be seen as the best is unquenchable. It's powerful. So powerful that they're willing to forsake their spouse and kids to have affairs with someone who will give them more active attention and make them look better (in their mind) than their spouse and kids do. Often this is someone more beautiful or handsome, better connected, wealthier, higher in social or career status, or politically connected. Maybe this person is you! And how wonderful, to feel so desired and desirable. But make no mistake, they will not stay faithful to you. Bottom line, their fear of feeling inferior doesn't allow them to feel content. Chasing the brass ring is never-ending.

Fake Protectiveness

Fake protectiveness is common with this personality. They want you to see them as big and strong, or as exciting and sexy. Both men and women with this personality are driven to be the life of the party—some with more success than others.

> *The reality is that I didn't feel protected, but there was a fantasy that was perpetuated that I would be protected. If I had paid attention and been honest with myself...I would have realized that no, I was not feeling protected. The truth is I was choosing to believe a fantasy. The bill I was being sold was that I was being protected. I wanted it to be real, but there was no alignment between what I was experiencing and reality.*

Their narcissism helps them rise to the top in business, in the dating world and other parts of life. Being in their circle or on their arm can seem fun and exciting because you feel a sense of security—and who doesn't like to hang out with fun people? But the fun is usually short-lived. The bubble will burst once the inferiority button is pushed. That immediately puts the narcissistic HCP operating system into full swing. The generous, chivalrous life of the party becomes a punishing jerk. A screaming meltdown with insults, personal attacks, and put-downs may ensue, and a not-so-quiet exit is guaranteed. They storm out of the room, slam the door. Eventually, you'll be not only unprotected but attacked.

Blind Spots Narcissists Can Hide In

Narcissists clearly spell trouble. So how is it that we end up in relationships with them? Let's look at some of the common blind spots that can make us vulnerable to this personality.

Low Self-Esteem

One is doubting your own judgment. Low self-esteem can make you more easily believe the show that a narcissist may be putting on for you. "Too good to be true" is a common experience with narcissists, yet if you have low self-esteem you may be so eager for attention and praise that you miss that it's all a manipulation. Your self-esteem rises as they treat you better and better—but once you're hooked, your self-esteem is crushed when they make you the target of their blame.

Many people in relationships with narcissists have told us that they initially felt in awe of their partner and felt inadequate beside them. Feeling low self-esteem around someone is sometimes a sign of a narcissist beside you.

Bill says that one sign of a narcissist for him is when he's driving home from the office and feels that he is really incompetent and in the wrong field. Then he thinks, *Wait a minute! Did I see a narcissist in my office today?* And the answer is always yes. This is a very common feeling around narcissists, because they try to soak up all the attention and importance in the room. The good news is that you are probably their equal, or even superior to them in your own abilities.

Megan has learned to recognize a similar reaction that tells her there's a narcissist in her radar field. At first, she enjoys talking with someone who seems fun and highly intelligent. But then her self-esteem takes a hit, and she starts to feel nervous, which causes her to talk too much. Within a short time, she can feel her batteries starting to drain.

You, too, can learn to recognize your own characteristic reaction to narcissists. For many people, it shows up as a brief wobble in self-esteem. The trick is to recognize it for what it is: a signal about someone else's personality, not your own worth.

Loneliness, Grief, or Shyness

Narcissists are skilled at "love-bombing" people with their positive attention. The initial meeting with a narcissist is so fantastic. The love and attention they shower on you is intoxicating. If you are lonely or grieving or shy, you are at risk of getting sucked in by a narcissist, because this is one of their greatest skills: making people feel good, important, and loved. But don't be fooled. This is just an act in the initial stage of their romances. It usually doesn't last for long—maybe six to twelve months at the most.

To check your blind spot, think about how they make you feel. If you initially feel safe and have the sense that a relationship with this person means you don't have to carry this burden called life all by yourself, then you might be vulnerable. You may interpret the controlling behavior of the narcissist as chivalrous, when in reality it's their unhealthy relationship operating system. They may follow you home after a date just to "make sure you got home okay." Don't mistake that for caring. It's creepy! What makes you feel safe today may be the end of your freedom. You may wake up in the night to find your narcissistic partner staring at you or hovering over you. That might be okay if your partner weren't a narcissist. But it may also be meant to intimidate you and weaken your sense of self, your security, and your resolve over time.

Anything that makes you feel alone or bad about yourself can develop into a blind spot. If you have trauma in your childhood (abuse, sexual abuse, neglect, emotional abuse), or you've had a parent with a personality disorder, or a past romantic partner with these behaviors, you are vulnerable. You are at risk.

It's tricky because you start out feeling great about yourself with the narcissistic partner, but you'll leave the relationship feeling as though you've lost a good part of yourself, and then you're forced to claw your way back from the loss and rebuild.

Believing You Can Change Them

Narcissists are almost always talking and teaching you their view of the world. If you have naïve beliefs about difficult people changing or being rescued by you, they will draw you in. Whether their story is an exciting one about how wonderful they are or a tragic one about how unfairly they have been treated, you are at risk of believing that you can change them or help them become a better person.

One contributor reported this about her experiences in romantic relationships with two different narcissists:

He led with who he was and it was valid—he'd gained status as a national celebrity in the entertainment industry. Being on his arm was wonderful and stimulating. We went to amazing events and met interesting, talented celebrities. He loved showing me off. It was always fun and it made me feel special, like I'd joined a unique club. Early in the relationship, after the uber-charming phase, he told me about all the famous women he'd dated in the past. I thought, "Wow, I'm supposed to feel really special, right? He's including me in a small club of impressive people and he's trusting me with this information." That's kind of how it was pitched, but that's not how it made me feel. Instead, it made me feel really insecure. In the back of my head I thought, "Gee, I'm really lucky." That's where the manipulation came in, but it was based in reality, based in truth. A complete mind-distorter.

Looking back, wondering why I was so vulnerable, I now see that the manipulation was utilized in a way that combined with my own insecurities to create a perfect storm.

What I learned in my second relationship with a narcissist was quite the opposite. So much of the stuff that he told me was real was, in actuality, just grandiose b.s. He came across as ultrasensitive to what had happened in my other relationship. Saying what I wanted to hear. It was complete and utter fabrication with just enough of the appearance of reality that I was buying it at first. I started smelling it pretty quickly but I kept pretty quiet about it. I just didn't say anything, but my instincts screamed the entire time until the gaslighting started right in front me. I held it together until I could leave. He was always selling himself. You think it's all about you, but it's really all about them. They're priming you so you can feed it back to them. This is what they breathe.

What I learned overall is that my family of origin made me vulnerable to narcissists. I had to examine why I was so absolutely attracted to them.

Some narcissists present themselves as empty and needy, which may make you want to protect them and make them into better people. But what they're really doing is attaching to you. They're not a full molecule—they're seeking to be whole. They look like they're loving and caring, but once you're with them, there comes a point when they go back to their permanent patterns once again. They're Oscar-worthy actors. It looks like one thing, but it's another. And then you're stuck.

Think you can change this pattern? Think again. Many try, but actually feel worse afterward, because rather than changing, the narcissist remains the same and resists your efforts by belittling you. Until you realize that these patterns were embedded in the narcissist long ago—often in childhood (through abuse or entitlement)—you will waste your energy trying to help them and invite further ridicule. As one respondent said:

> *Saw signs of the red flags but didn't understand the consequences of ignoring them.*

Quiz: Are You Dating a Narcissist HCP?

Here's an informal quiz. It's not a scientific survey, but it can help you think about whether your partner might be a narcissistic HCP. You can also take this test online: **www.dating-radar.com.** Answer with a "1" for yes and "0" for no.

Your partner:

_____ Is charming in front of others but insults you in private.

_____ Gets angry and verbally insults you or others when they feel disrespected.

_____ Laughs at you, demeans you, mocks you, exposes and exploits your weaknesses in front of others or in private.

_____ Is verbally or physically abusive when they feel disrespected.

_____ Lies easily.

_____ Has to be in control and make the rules. (You have to ask permission or be "allowed" to go places, talk to people, and so on.)

_____ Talks about themselves more than listening to you. (Doesn't have interest in your life, or helping you pursue your dreams). Needs to constantly be in the spotlight.

_____ Feels entitled to be the boss; is never wrong; always has to be right.

_____ Sabotages positive attention paid to you, or sabotages your events; punishes you later.

_____ Expects you to sacrifice your needs, desires, and dreams.

_____ Accuses you of things they're actually doing; blames you.

_____ Cuts you off from family and friends.

_____ TOTAL

0	Green (mild)	Take the test again or ask a trusted friend for input, to be sure you're not missing something. If you get 0 again, go for it— but keep your eyes open.
1 - 2	Yellow (spicy)	Consider getting out now. If you're not ready to get out, proceed with caution.
3 - 12	Red (nuclear)	Don't commit to this person unless you're ready to sacrifice.

Conclusion

Narcissistic HCPs can be very appealing and seductive, but you can spot them if you know what to look for. Their warning signs include their belief that they are very superior and entitled to special treatment, combined with constant disdain for others they see as inferior.

These warning signs are not hard to see if you pay close attention to how they treat *other* people. But they work hard at jamming your radar using their charm *with you*, their strong appearance of protectiveness *for you*, and their exciting sexuality *with you*. Your own blind spots can make you particularly susceptible to narcissistic HCPs, because they work so hard at giving the appearance of taking care of you and being impressed with you. Yet for those who have made progress on reducing their own blind spots, this personality may be one of the easiest to recognize *because* they are so obviously absorbed in looking good and telling you how wonderful they are.

They may entice you with who they know, what they've done, how smart they are, and where they've been. It's exciting and alluring…at first. But that bubble will burst. While your purpose early on may be primarily to make them look good to others, or get access to others, they will soon become very demeaning. They live in a fantasy world of winners and losers, so sooner or later you will become a loser in their eyes—a handy target of blame. The highest highs will predict the lowest lows.

CHAPTER FIVE

Don't Be Blindsided by a Borderline!

"You can live without them; they can't live without you."

Core Fear – Being Abandoned

The word *blindsided* couldn't be more accurate when it comes to dating a borderline HCP. They are incredible romantic partners in the beginning, but eventually another side comes out, catching you completely by surprise. It becomes apparent that they are dependent on being with or near you to feel okay. This change can happen gradually, over time. Often, the dynamic reveals itself once the relationship is seen as permanent.

In this chapter, we'll describe the borderline HCP's pattern of dating and relationship behavior, the ways they jam your radar, and the blind spots that make you vulnerable to falling in love with them. Just as you read in chapter 4 that not everyone who has narcissistic personality disorder has a high-conflict personality, the same applies to those with borderline personality disorder. It's only a subset of people with personality disorders who also have high-conflict personalities—those with *targets of blame*. Many people with this painful disorder are able to have successful relationships and are great parents. And borderline personality disorder seems to be the one of the four discussed in this book to have the most successful treatment outcomes for those who seek it. In this book, we are talking only about those who truly have the high-conflict personality pattern of behavior described in chapter 1.

So what is borderline personality disorder? People with borderline personalities are constantly fearful of being abandoned, and they have extreme mood swings and sudden, intense anger. This is a potent mix, which may lie under the surface of many sweet, charming, intelligent and attractive dates—male or female. Most people describe not knowing what hit them when this surprise personality finally comes out.

It's confusing. What once seemed like the perfect relationship turns into a nightmare at lightning speed. It can feel like a classic bait and switch. The sweet person who quickly stole your heart, just as quickly becomes needy. They have to be attached to you in some way all the time in order to feel okay. The amazing person who seems to be your perfect match can instantly go into a rage. It's scary for the target of blame—the person on the receiving end of this rage—and sometimes for the person having the rage.

Think of it this way: borderline HCPs have an absolute requirement to feel attached to at least one person all the time (think of them as super clingy). In most cases their object of attachment is a romantic interest. Once they're attached, they need to stay attached, no matter what. When they feel even slightly disconnected from that person, this overwhelming anxiety must be relieved ASAP and by any means necessary, as with HCPs in general; hence the bad behavior. They need to feel okay again. Instead of logically thinking through options to *calm* anxiety, they do the opposite, which is to *express* it forcefully, maybe even desperately. This is a recipe for mood swings and intense anger.

Borderline HCPs don't want to be this way. It's just how their operating system is programmed to work. The strange part is that, like other HCPs, most do not know why they operate this way. It's how they've developed throughout their lifetime. It feels normal and necessary. So they don't know any different, and they don't see how their operating system works against their best interests by making them so disagreeable that their partners end up avoiding them.

The temptation is to blast them back with anger and frustration, or try to fix or help them. But that never solves the problem and frequently makes things worse. They can get angrier than you ever can. Just watch!

Rage is the term commonly associated with borderlines. And their "abandonment rage" has inspired authors since Shakespeare penned his famous phrase "Hell hath no fury like a woman scorned." Of course, we have learned that this phrase can equally apply to borderline men.

Recognizing this pattern sometimes can take six to twelve months, although signs of it usually occur much earlier. While you might be tempted to immediately break up with them in an angry confrontation, it's usually best to maintain your own calm demeanor and respectfully ease out of the dating relationship once you've figured out what's going on.

As with the other HCP types, needy behavior occurs on a continuum from mild to nuclear. Some people have just a few traits, and not extreme ones; others fall on the full-blown personality disorder end of the spectrum. In this case, the disorder in question is borderline personality disorder, or BPD.

The prevalence of this personality disorder is almost 6

percent, according to the large National Institutes of Health study (Grant et al. 2008). Add to this the many people who just have *traits* of this disorder, and you have a substantial percent of the dating pool to watch out for. That study found that there is some overlap of people with borderline personality disorder and people with narcissistic personality disorder, so don't be surprised if someone seems to have warning signs of both. Also, those who may have these disorders need to be aware that they may be attracted to others with these disorders. So you'll want to be able to spot this type of HCP.

Let's look at the relationship patterns to watch out for. We'll talk about how borderline HCPs can jam your radar and then how your own blind spots may pull you toward someone with this exciting, but possibly dangerous or damaging, personality.

Fear Factor: Abandonment

The borderline HCP is driven by a fear of being abandoned. To them, it seems as if they have no option other than to feel attached all of the time.

What makes them feel abandoned?

1. Anything that makes them feel disconnected from you
2. Your absence (leaving for work or the gym, for example)
3. Not hearing from you while you're away
4. Your phone calls, time spent on social media, anything that connects you with other people
5. Turning your back to them in bed or walking away from them during an argument
6. Not including them in discussions, conversations, or event planning

7. A condescending or disapproving tone of voice—or one that they perceive this way
8. Being interrupted
9. Your relationships with other people (not all, just those that feel threatening to your relationship)
10. Prenuptial agreements (the idea that the relationship might end feels like a death sentence for them)

Borderline HCP
FEAR OF BEING **ABANDONED**
Overly friendly Shifts to anger Sudden mood swings
Needs to be **attached**

Their sensitivities are constantly gathering and assessing information for threats to their attachment to you. They need to be in your presence, in some way. This might be actual physical presence or through electronic means like texting. Their tolerance for separation is tested when they don't know where you are, or even have the thought that you might be unreachable.

Also, they are sensitive to a person's tone of voice; a tone that they perceive as negative sends them into instant panic. They also react strongly to facial expressions and other body language. The moment any feeling of abandonment is triggered, borderline HCPs must do whatever it takes to feel attached again. They have to react to the threat before it destroys them. They don't really have any flexibility in how they respond. And they don't have much self-awareness, either. They're programmed this way, but they don't know it.

The unfortunate part is that when they're triggered, they do the opposite of what you'd expect. Instead of reacting to you with sweetness and sugar in an attempt to reattach, they react aggressively. Like narcissists, they don't think before pulling the emotional trigger. They shoot accusations first—and then they feel better, because their anxiety begins to calm once the feeling of intense connection fills them once again. Ironically, even though their intention is to strengthen the bond, the angry outbursts ultimately sabotage the relationship. You will be frustrated, exhausted, or annoyed.

It's important to emphasize that although people with borderline personality disorder or borderline traits have fear of abandonment as a core issue, not everyone with a borderline personality is an HCP. Some turn inward, taking their anxieties out on themselves, while others turn their anxieties externally onto their next target of blame. It's the outward-facing borderline HCPs that you really need to watch out for as relationship partners. This doesn't mean that they can't or don't get better or that they can't be part of a healthy relationship at some point, but they need specific treatment first.

Roller Coaster Love

"After my long, drawn out divorce, it took a while before I was ready to start dating again, and it had been twenty-five years since I'd last been on a date. I was surprised how many went out with me. A few didn't work out for whatever reason. And then I met Jessa. She was fifteen years younger (about the same age as my son), gorgeous, and smart. We were compatible with each other's life dreams, goals, likes, and dislikes, all the way down to our favorite foods and the fact that we were both "night people" and didn't like mornings. I had a busy work schedule, so I was relieved to have a girlfriend whose work life was just as busy as mine. She wasn't needy. We were able to have a serious relationship without the pressures of my past relationships—women who needed a lot

more of my time. Jessa just adapted so easily.

We had a spark that was unmatched in my previous relationships. We were drunk with love. After about a month she began staying at my house one or two nights a week, and by the second month she was there full-time. This presented a problem. I was a study leader at my church, and they didn't approve of living together outside of marriage. But I was falling in love with this girl, so church would just have to take a back seat. I deluded myself into thinking I could keep it hidden.

Then Jessa lost her job, which meant she was at home all day and ready for lots of interaction when I arrived home at the end of an exhausting day. She'd get mad if I didn't want to go out or I didn't pay enough attention to her. The happy-go-lucky girl was becoming needy, pouty, and more and more demanding.

I started finding empty vodka bottles hidden around the house. Then the accusations of cheating started. Who was I on the phone with? Who had I talked to today? Where did I go to lunch? When I wouldn't tell her, she gave me the silent treatment and said I'd be lucky to ever have sex again but maybe my ex-wife would pony up. Accusations turned into fights. Fights turned into rage fests. At some point, object throwing began. Whatever was in her hand was going to zing my past ear, or hit my head, or the wall or the floor. And the F word flew out of her mouth like verbal vomit. She'd lock herself in the bathroom, saying she was going to drown herself in the bathtub. I knew she had vodka in there, so when I heard water running in the bathtub, I'd frantically try to get in but I couldn't get through the door. So I'd keep her talking through the door and eventually coax her out with promises that I wouldn't talk to so-and-so, or go certain places. She'd wilt like a child…sometimes apologizing.

My life was suddenly hell. My job required travel, but how could I leave her alone? She needed constant minding. What if she went through with her threats to kill herself? She threatened it constantly. I canceled as many trips as I could, sending my employees instead, until one trip came up that I couldn't neglect—the executives meeting held before the annual shareholders meeting of our publicly traded company. There was no getting out of this one, so before flying off to Las Vegas I did everything possible to make sure she knew I was coming back the next day, and assured her that I would call her when I could and she could call if she needed to. That was a huge mistake. Instead of the hundred calls I expected, there was radio silence, except for one solitary text saying she'd also flown to Las Vegas and checked into a hotel where she would end her life. When I tried calling her, no answer. I texted, no response. I had to present my report to the executives, but stepped out every chance I could get to track her down. No one can imagine the terror and panic I felt, knowing I was the only one who could save her. But she'd bluffed in the past, so now I had to decide whether to take her seriously, leave the meeting, and risk losing my job—or risk having her death on my conscience the rest of my life.

I called all the hotels in Las Vegas that I knew she'd previously stayed. She was at none of them. This was the worst day of my life. I called her friends, her family, her hairdresser, everyone I could think of, but no one had heard from her. The one place I hadn't thought to check was home. When I got home that night, there she was, sitting on the couch in my living room.

This was my life for a while—rage, drinking, suicide threats. But she was also sometimes sweet, soft, and extremely sensitive.

I felt like a parent and a minder, not a boyfriend. My life became a world of opposites. She changed her mind constantly, keeping me chasing my tail. When I finally made up my mind to end the relationship, she went ballistic. She called for an ambulance, saying she had overdosed. When they arrived, it didn't take them long to figure out nothing was wrong with her. Completely drained and stuck in a hole so deep I didn't think I'd ever get out, I left the house and checked into a hotel.

She called or texted me—no joke—every thirty seconds for hours. The next day, she started a series of calls to my boss and every member of the board of directors, accusing me of using company funds for personal use. She demanded that they fire me and take away my stock options, retirement account, and "everything financial." Next, she emailed my parents, my sister, and my son to expose my "sexual secrets." She sent an extraordinarily long email to the minister at my church and several of my close friends there, telling them we'd been living together and having sex. All the while, she continued sending me confusing texts—threats of harming herself mixed with pleas like "Let's stick together— we can work this out." I finally went to the court and got a restraining order to keep her away from me at my work, but that didn't stop the texts and emails. I was able to salvage my work relationships, but only after going through a thorough an internal investigation that cost the company financially and me personally. I had to do a lot of damage control. I stepped down from my position at the church and, I have to admit, my family will never look at me the same way again.

Just as suddenly as she'd entered my life, she disappeared. No more texts. No more emails. No more calls. I heard through the grapevine that she had met someone new.

This relationship began with an unprecedented spark, a classic HCP warning sign. She jammed his radar with fake compatibility. Then she became completely dependent on him for social interaction. Before long, the two of them were locked in a cycle of accusations of infidelity, threats of suicide, and desperate attempts at reconnection. The downward spiral ended with his life in ruins.

Chris the Gentleman

I fell in love with Chris. He was a gentleman, which is hard to find these days. He opened doors, walked beside instead of in front of me like other guys, and was just about the sweetest person I'd ever met. Almost too sweet, but we also had great chemistry. Great chemistry! And amazing sex! We got married within three months.

Over the next few months I began noticing some strange behaviors. He would call me or text me dozens of times a day. At first, it seemed sweet, but then it started to come off as kind of desperate. During times I wasn't available, he would find someone else to "chat" with. It was like he couldn't be alone for a single second.

After a while, his constant checking up on me began to seem downright controlling. We fought over the time I spent on Facebook or talking to my friends or family on the phone, or any time I didn't give him 100 percent of my attention. I complied just to keep things smooth, but it got annoying and scary. He was a big guy. My friends and family thought I was nuts for staying with him. In hindsight, those relationships suffered terribly during that time.

Why did I stay? Plain and simple, it was empathy for his past and hope that things would get better for us with time. If I could give him enough empathy about his neglectful and abusive childhood and do things his way, he would get better. If I could somehow reassure him that I was really there for him, maybe he would back off a little. He promised to go to counseling but insisted it had to be couples counseling because, he said, I had just as big a problem as he did. I loved this guy so much and I didn't believe in divorce.

Meanwhile, my life was hell. I felt like I was in a deep, dark hole with no escape. But if I let him go, what would become of him? I was sure he would fall apart if I left now. So the logical decision was to try counseling and commit to helping this person who had little ability to help himself. I didn't want to be responsible for his breakdown—or worse, his death, if he followed through on his threats to jump off a bridge.

My health was deteriorating and I suppose my mental toughness was, too. And then it got even messier when I realized he had an opiate problem. Now, on top of everything else, I was stuck with a drug addict. Now I really couldn't leave, or he would migrate from opiates to heroin and he would die.

So I stayed far too long. I felt used and exhausted. My life was chaos. I tried leaving a few times, once, before we were engaged, which is how I ended up engaged to him. The minute I told him I was breaking it off, he produced an engagement ring, proposed to me, and begged me to stay with him forever.

We've been divorced a long time now. He's lived with several different women and been married several times.

What's Special about Borderline HCPs?

People on the borderline personality continuum suffer from a fear of abandonment that often dates back to very early childhood. They didn't ask to have these problems. In many cases, they may not have experienced the security of a stable parent-child relationship, so they didn't learn how to regulate their emotions. Borderline personality can also stem from childhood trauma, or even trauma occurring in adulthood.

And some people are just born this way, regardless of good parenting. They might have been thought of as the overly sensitive child in the family. For some people, it's a mix of factors. The combination of genetics that lean toward higher emotional sensitivity and the insecurities that come from bad parenting is a significant predictor of the borderline operating system. Bottom line, it's an unwanted visitor.

The borderline brain goes to extremes to feel connected. This drive toward attachment is a powerful force. For many people with borderline personalities, this desperate need for security may cause them to turn to food or drugs or sex. These often become addictions with a new set of problems. In fact, all of the personality disorders mentioned in this book have a higher incidence of addictions. The two examples above help demonstrate this.

Borderlines may pick arguments and behave in controlling ways until their partner gets fed up and leaves. Then they desperately want to reattach. If the partner isn't available, they may drive across the country back to their parents. Of course, they probably don't have a peaceful relationship with their family, either, so their parents are shocked when the son or daughter who left in a huff years ago—or whom they'd taken a break from—has driven nonstop across the country to be with them.

Borderline HCPs fear abandonment so profoundly that they want to be connected at any cost. Since it seems essential to be in a relationship and to stay in it, their brain is always on the lookout for threats to their connection to you. But they don't apply this schema very consistently. For example, they may be entirely comfortable with your parents' presence in your life, but despise your sister and do everything in their power to get you to separate yourself from her. Or it could a friend, a job, or a hobby—anything that, in their mind, might compete with your connection with them.

It's in the borderline HCPs threat mode that you'll see mood swings. Their day may be going along just fine until you get a text that they suspect is from their perceived threat. Before you can blink, their internal anxiety goes from zero to sixty, and the race is on. The storm starts raging and hits you before you even heard the forecast. From loving to angry. From calm to nuclear. From a peaceful drive to road rage.

They will pull out all the stops to stay attached, even if it's entirely sacrificial for them and to their detriment. Their misguided connection-seeking behavior may seem irrational to you, but it's more than logical to them. They feel the need for attachment so intensely that they cannot be swayed from it. They will stay in relationships that are bad for them and maybe even harmful. It looks bizarre from the outside, but not from the inside of the borderline mind.

Borderline HCPs swing—sometimes very rapidly— between very friendly and very angry. This can occur within a matter of minutes. Because of this volatility, it can really feel like you're on a roller coaster. The friendly, loving, sweet person who uses heart emojis in abundance in one text can deliver another that makes you feel a chill of shock and dread. It feels like you've just been bitten by a snake—which is why we call it "being fanged." On the other hand, just when you think that they hate you and are out the door, they just as suddenly become friendly again, as though nothing happened. This helps explain the title of one of the most popular books on this subject: *I Hate You! Don't Leave Me!*

Sadly, for some borderline HCPs, the power of attachment overrides all logic and drives them to the point that they're in so much pain that they have to seek relief in whatever way is most convenient in the moment. It may be jumping out of a moving car, drinking, taking drugs, or self-harming through cutting, head-banging, or other destructive behaviors. The pain becomes so intolerable that they feel they have to do something extreme just to survive.

Some will take it out on you as a target of blame—destroying your property, calling your friends to expose your worst secrets, defacing your car. While these actions may be driven by pain, it can also be vindictiveness or revenge. When they feel like they're out of options, revenge may be their last resort—anything to escape the pain, even temporarily.

It's important to understand that people with this personality are in an almost constant state of fear, just trying to keep their head above water. Think of your own fears and the anxiety, or even panic, they can create. If you felt that way most of the time, your life would be very different. People with borderline personalities are continually in a lot of emotional pain that they don't understand. They're just trying to survive it.

However, at the core, they think (actually, they are certain) that they're bad. If your partner says "You think I'm bad," or "Well, I guess I'm just an awful person," then you may be dealing with someone with this type of personality. They're actually begging you to tell them "You're not bad," "You're not an awful person," but by that point you're so annoyed or frustrated that you want to run from the room or hang up the phone. Threats of self-harm or suicide are also common with borderline HCPs. What they're really saying is, "Please tell me I shouldn't hurt myself; please tell me I shouldn't kill myself."

When their pleas are ignored, they feel like they're drowning. They need a bandage to stop the bleed, and you're in possession of the bandage, the only one who can apply it. Your innocent suggestion may feel like criticism to them, which makes them instantly react aggressively toward you.

They attach so quickly. Move in quickly. Insert themselves in your life in a way that makes it hard to get them out. They pull on your heartstrings and good nature to stay in the relationship so they won't fall apart. But you cannot heal them, and the relationship will never be entirely healthy. Think of it this way: having undetected cancer works against your body. Eventually it will take over your body if left untreated. In the same way, this personality type is going to take over your mind and your life if you don't recognize it.

The good news is that there are therapies that can really help many of those with borderline personality disorder or milder versions of this problem. These treatments include dialectical behavior therapy (DBT) and other cognitive behavioral therapies. The bad news is that most people with borderline personality disorder don't seem to have any interest in getting treatment. It's partly because they don't know that they need help. Remember that lack of self-awareness is a hallmark of personality problems. And another defining feature of personality disorders is blaming other people. So they may decide that their difficulties are someone else's fault—maybe yours.

Key Characteristics

Here are the classic patterns of borderline HCPs in "love" relationships. Note that we are talking about people with borderline personality disorder *and* those with just some traits.

1. They see the world in all-or-nothing terms; people are all good or all bad.
2. They see themselves as sometimes all good (at least compared to certain other people) and sometimes all bad.
3. They tend to see others as all good at first, until they suddenly see them as all bad.
4. They have trouble regulating their emotions. They vacillate from extreme highs to extreme lows with little in between. They feel intense love, intense sadness, and intense anger.
5. They may go through periods of depression (feeling helpless or hopeless, feeling weighted down, having trouble concentrating and making decisions, and so on) or agitated depression (some of those same negative feelings, but combined with restlessness instead of feelings of heaviness).
6. They can be indirect—hinting at what is important to them, or hinting that they might hurt themselves. They

may seem manipulative, making extreme threats and then forgetting or retracting or denying them.

7. Even after extremely negative emotions and behavior, they can switch back to being friendly and loving (for a while).

8. They need to feel included or welcome in your life at all times. They cling to their partners and to their children. They can be very possessive, checking up constantly on their family members.

9. They involve many other people in their disputes, including their children, other relatives, coworkers, friends, professionals, and so on. They "split" friends, children, coworkers and others against each other.

10. They often involve others in their anger, including publicly attacking them by spreading rumors (also known as "distortion campaigns") and sometimes publicly making serious false allegations of abuse.

11. They have sudden and intense rage, which sometimes includes violence; then it may be totally gone the next day. But it usually returns.

12. Many have high-conflict divorces, including extreme custody battles over the children.

Given their numbers, you probably have met or even dated someone with these personality characteristics by now. Most of the traits are self-explanatory, but we want to say more about the last five (8–12).

Splitting

Just like narcissistic HCPs, borderline HCPs tend to see people in extremes: as all good or all bad. For borderline HCPs, the split is often between people who are trustworthy or caring and those who they see as out to get them, those who they think are evil and engage in the worst behavior. They often will discuss other people with you in those terms, and demand absolute loyalty from you. Then, when they perceive that you have been less than perfect at that, they will turn on you and consider you to be one of the worst human beings alive. This can be quite jolting.

But at some point the fear of losing you will creep back in, so they may turn on the charm again and try to draw you back into the relationship. Some people call this "hoovering"—like a Hoover vacuum cleaner sucking you back in. This tends to happen over and over again, so partners often feel as if they're going crazy, when in fact the dynamic is a predictable yo-yo, up-and-down, part of the borderline pattern. In fact, there is a book, by Paul Mason and Randi Kreger, which talks about this pattern, titled *Stop Walking on Eggshells,* because that is what it feels like.

Being attached is like oxygen for a borderline HCP. When they feel a threat to the attachment, they feel as if they can't breathe. So they get angry because they feel you're detaching (even if you're not), and push hard to get you to admit it. Once you've had enough and threaten to leave, they do whatever it takes to get you back in, to once again feel attached and feel as if they can breathe again.

Here's what two of our survey respondents said:

...repeated abandonment and hoovering.

Being extra nice and then "disappearing" for a couple of days afterward. Being idealized and then devalued.

Disturbingly, many people with this personality who are

parents see their children in split terms as well: they see one child as extremely good (the one who tends to do most of what they want and serves as an ally in that parent's battles) and the other child as extremely bad (the one who may be more emotionally removed from the parent or openly oppositional). Both types of children are extremely stressed by this type of behavior—being pulled into adult disputes and being compared all the time.

> *My eleven-year-old daughter, who'd endured her mom and me fighting for her entire life, finally said, "I wish one of you would just die so there wouldn't be any more fighting."*

Domestic Violence

Coercive controlling violence, the most severe type of domestic violence,[1] is known for one partner trying to have power and control over the other partner, who lives with ongoing fear and sometimes broken bones or other injuries. Most commonly, from our observations and family court experience, it is a borderline man trying to control his female partner with verbal abuse, physical abuse, sexual abuse, total financial control, and isolation her from family and friends. Sometimes this possessiveness

---

1 *Other types of domestic violence include (Kelly and Johnson 2008):* **Situation couple violence,** *which usually involves both partners engaging in pushing and shoving from time to time because of a lack of conflict resolution skills. Usually there isn't a pattern of power and control, or fear or injuries, and it may be that neither person has a high-conflict personality.* **Separation-instigated violence,** *which usually involves one or two incidents around the time of separation, without a pattern of power and control, or fear or injuries, and it may be that neither person has a high-conflict personality.* **Violent resistance,** *which occurs when a victim of coercive controlling violence tries to fight back to protect themselves. On rare occasions this may lead to the death of the perpetrator of the coercive violence, but more often it leads to serious injuries for the victim who fights back. For more information or help, go to The National Domestic Violence Hotline: www.thehotline.org or 1-800-799-7233.*

results in death. The person is trying to have extreme control over their environment, because they feel so out of control inside.

We've seen a few cases involving a woman as the perpetrator of this same behavior toward her male partner, as well as same-sex relationships in which one person is using violence for power and control over the other. The pattern is the same.

Most commonly, this borderline domestic violence pattern has three phases: 1) an internal buildup of abandonment fear and anger; 2) an outburst of rage—verbal, physical, or both; and 3) a period of remorse and promises to never do that again. But since it's a lack of self-regulation of emotions and behavior, it does happen again—and again. We call this the *cycle of violence*.

She would throw anything she was holding when she snapped...a plate of food, the remote control. She'd scratch my back, drawing blood, when I turned my back to her in bed.

I came out of an abusive background, and his showers of affection were more than I'd ever had from anyone, even though they were interspersed with moments of aggression, disdain, and withholding affection.

She'd throw her wedding and engagement ring on the ground, and then we'd have to spend a lot of time looking for them.

Possessiveness and Jealousy

Once you are in a committed relationship with someone with a borderline personality, they often become overly preoccupied with keeping you in the relationship. They are constantly testing you, to see if you really care, will really stick by them, will really love them despite their challenging behavior. They cling (calling you at work a lot, showing up at work, continuously contacting you when you're with your friends). And then they go into a rage if they think you are straying from them (having an affair, thinking of splitting up, or just coming home late from work). If you've never experienced this kind of behavior before, it can be quite surprising. Partners of borderline HCPs often spend a lot of time explaining and defending their ordinary actions.

Seeing my family became too stressful. He felt abandoned if I even wanted to go to lunch with my brother.

...couldn't invite my best friend to our wedding because she was so jealous of him. I decided to invite him at the last minute, which put her in a tailspin and ruined our wedding.

I finally closed my social media accounts because she insisted on seeing everything, including texts and voicemail. If I didn't let her see it, she'd figure out my passwords and read everything anyway.

I've even moved my daughter from our home to ease our anxiety from the stalking.

High-Conflict Divorce

We have both assisted people going through difficult divorces with partners who have patterns of behavior that seem to fit those of borderline personality disorder. In fact, this is the personality that shows up most often in the inquiries we get regarding difficult divorces. Bill and Randi Kreger wrote a book to address these concerns, titled *Splitting: Protecting Yourself While Divorcing Someone with Borderline or Narcissistic Personality Disorder.*

When a borderline HCP ends up in family court, the custody battle often can be extremely bitter. Borderline HCPs may see the partner in ideal terms at the start of the relationship, but if their partners divorce them, they often switch to seeing them as all bad (see number 3 above). So they fight for complete control of the children and try to shut out the other parent, or at least minimize their contact with the children. These custody battles sometimes go on for years (partly because the courts don't understand them at first).

He was financially very harsh to me during our separation.

Divorcing and coparenting with a high-conflict person is difficult, and counseling support is imperative to make it through.

After three years of separation he still hates me, but thankfully, we parent well, as I try really hard regardless of his behavior.

Be aware that when the relationship finishes, you will experience the divorce from hell.

False Allegations

Whether you become involved in a high-conflict divorce or not, having a relationship with a high-conflict person who has borderline personality disorder or traits seems to increase the likelihood that you will be the target of false allegations. Often these relate to improper sexual behavior, physical abuse, taking or controlling money, treating children badly, or some other bad behavior.

You may notice that these behaviors are similar to the actual abusive behaviors that some borderlines engage in, such as domestic violence. The flip side is that this same general personality pattern involves making false allegations of abusive behavior. Sometimes, the same person who is *actually* engaging in abusive behavior makes false allegations that *you* are engaging in such behavior.

If you start seeing signs of abusive behavior or false allegations, be very careful to avoid confrontations, and seek the advice of a qualified lawyer or counselor.

> *He filed a restraining order against me two weeks after I fled home. He made false allegations about me. He got sole physical custody. Despite a visitation order, I am not able to see my children because he won't bring them for visitation. The kids say they don't want to see me. He has turned them against me. He does not want me to be in my children's lives.*

> *Didn't marry or move in but relationship lasted two-and-a-half years. Red flags were really lengthy emails from the person, which were typically filled with veiled accusations of cheating or blaming regarding simple to major grievances. The emails would come out of the blue when I would be unaware the other person was unhappy. The emails were never preceded with conversation.*

This surprise-attack mode seems common for high-conflict people, who are constantly blaming and making allegations of cheating or something similar. It's also common that someone with this pattern acts as if you know what they are thinking and suddenly blasts you with complaints as though they were in the middle of a conversation that you knew about all along. Jealousy, indirect manipulation (sulking, silence) and false allegations can become chronic in such a relationship.

By the Numbers

In answer to the question:

Would you consider your partner (or former partner) to have traits of one of the following personality disorders?

Approximately 20 percent of the respondents said

borderline personality disorder. But over 26 percent said they saw traits of *both* borderline and narcissistic personality disorder. In those cases, people were dealing with someone who had the difficulties of a narcissistic personality described in chapter 4, plus the difficulties described above.

Here is a survey comment that describes what it's like to be in a relationship with a high-conflict person who also has borderline personality disorder:

This person was quick to anger. He had a Dr. Jekyll/Mr Hyde personality, signs of a controlling personality. He wanted to be with me 24/7, and was quick in wanting to lock me down to a commitment. He was possessive, displayed extreme jealousy, and was passive/aggressive. His personality changed rapidly from being the perfect gentlemen to being a mean, unpredictable person. He eventually became a mentally and verbally abusive partner, and ultimately physically abusive. I have learned that these types of people can hide these personality disorders very well. They are very intelligent and extremely manipulative. There are clear signs once you remove yourself from these toxic relationships and educate yourself on how innocent people (most of the time women) are manipulated into being in relationships with these types of men, often without even realizing that they are being manipulated, controlled, and—much worse—abused.

We want to comment that from our experience and observations, men are just as often manipulated into these relationships as women. The big difference is that male borderline HCPs seem to be more likely to be physically abusive, whereas female borderline HCPs seem to be more likely to make public false allegations of a variety of abusive behavior—although both men and women engage in both kinds of behavior. The big NIH study mentioned at the beginning of the chapter found that 47 percent of those with borderline personality disorder were men and 53 percent were women (Grant et al. 2008). This is interesting, because in the past (including in the *DSM-IV* from 1994), women were considered to make up three-quarters of those with this disorder.

How Borderline HCPs Jam Your Radar

You'd think that such profound personality problems would be evident right from the start, but like all HCPs, borderline HCPs have ways of keeping their troubles under wraps long enough to reel you in. After all, they're desperate to be in a relationship, so it makes sense that they would have developed some strategies to keep things pleasant long enough to get a commitment from you. Let's take a look at how to jam your radar.

Charm

In the beginning, borderline HCPs mostly jam your radar with lots and lots of charm. They feel empty without a relationship, so they need to market their best self to attract you and attach to you. They can be very exciting, affectionate, and emotionally engaging. There's typically lots of love-bombing right from the start. They often express that they are in awe of you—telling you how wonderful you are, how you draw out the best in them and make them a better person. They can be very attractive and seductive.

Even though borderline HCPs really turn on the charm at the beginning, it doesn't last. And the romantic partner is the person most likely to experience the most intense borderline behaviors; other people may never see it. Friends and family—

even psychologists—are often surprised when they learn that someone they know has this disorder. The person seemed so fun, charming, intelligent, witty, engaging! But since it's all about intimate attachment, borderline HCPs act out their worst fears with the people closest to them, so it may remain unnoticed by less intimate friends and family until they see a pattern or find out the person is in jail for domestic violence.

...had that "Prince Charming" quality. He wanted to take care of me and be my knight in shining armor.

He often talked about how special my love was, that my love was saving him.

Ticked all the boxes in terms of opening doors, being a gentleman.

Fake Compatibility

Borderline HCPs have their own brand of fake compatibility that comes from a unique personality trait, which is that they often have an unstable sense of self. Since their own identity doesn't feel stable, they may adopt some aspect of your identity in order to feel more grounded and closer to you. This may take the form of clothing style, hairstyle, musical interests, and so on. You may hear them talking passionately about a pastime that they have very recently acquired. They may truly like sharing your interests, even though they didn't have them before.

There's a second variation on fake compatibility to watch out for. Borderline HCPs may be super accommodating at first—for instance, always making themselves available to fit your schedule.

The person initially, for a short time, seemed to take interest in things that were important to me or people who were close me.

The interest quickly changed after the relationship had solidified.

It seemed that she was the perfect partner, always supportive and easy to get along with.

She loved everything I loved…hobbies, food, people, music. This included matching her schedule to mine, being available all the time, completely accommodating. Later I found out most of it wasn't true and it was actually the exact opposite of reality.

They generally are very sincere at first, and their sweetness can be very enticing. This may be totally honest on their part. It's just that they need to maintain that connection to you in order to manage their emotions.

Overt Sexuality

Borderline HCPs find reassurance and safety in a close physical relationship. They can be overtly flirtatious and sexual in the very beginning, even if they say they aren't. Many people with this disorder experienced sexual abuse in childhood, which in some adults leads to strong sexuality as a learned way to please a partner and create a strong bond or attachment.

Beware. Their sexual connection to you may be very sincere at the beginning, but sex is often used as a tool to keep you in the relationship when they fear abandonment. When they feel you slipping away, even if they're intensely angry at you, they can easily reattach through sexuality. This is the personality we most often hear about as difficult to split up with because the sex is so good. It's back and forth, love/hate, get away from you/come back to you. You may find yourself having "breakup sex" over and over again. For them, they end up with a lot of shame.

During our first dinner date, she said she didn't sleep around, but she started kissing me intimately and passionately—very sexually—in the parking lot beside her car. We slept together that night.

Unfortunately, we also hear repeatedly that sex was abundant before the relationship became solidified and almost nonexistent after.

Promising or Demanding Protection

Protection is often part of the dynamic, but borderline HCPs are more likely to demand it than to promise it. Borderline HCP men may say they will be protective when they really want or need to be taken care of instead. Borderline HCP women often seek to be protected and taken care of like a child by a parent. But then they make endless demands that can't be fulfilled. There's a classic Sheryl Crow song that seems to be exactly about this, with the refrain: *"Are you strong enough to be my man?"* If someone ever asks you that, that's a warning sign.

Beware being told that you *have to* take care of them. Borderline HCPs speak this way sometimes and many partners have felt hooked in and unable to withdraw when these kinds of excessive needs are expressed. In one case, a man told his girlfriend that he wanted to split up, but she said she had just found out she was pregnant. He decided to do the "honorable" thing and marry her right away and have the child. Except... there was no child! She wasn't pregnant at all. But she avoided feeling abandoned. Because he wanted to honor his commitment, he stayed a long time. But eventually he got divorced.

Here are two examples from the survey:

Every time we were about to break up, she said her period was late. It was like clockwork. Turns out she wasn't able to get pregnant and knew it before we met.

My heart said no but my boundaries were not respected, from about our third date. When I tried to break off the engagement he cried and sobbed and said he could not live without me. I had grown up as an overly responsible child with parental dysfunction so I felt responsible for his feelings.

Experienced very high highs—quite manic in his excitement to be with me. To very low lows, where he didn't want me to be around him. He would warn me that he is not a very good person. He didn't really have any friends and had a very poor relationship with his family. I hadn't thought much of this initially, as he presented himself as the victim when he explained those relationships. My understanding of the situation changed as I met his family further along during our relationship.

Some borderlines do promise protection rather than demand it.

Attentive, caring, interested, concerned for my welfare. Flattering. Adulation despite my repeated insistence that I did not want to be placed on a pedestal because I believe in equal footing in any relationship.

Sometimes protective. It was the initial dream of how well he treated me in the beginning that I hoped would come back.

Both of these survey respondents replied *no* to the question: *Would you have entered into a relationship with this person if you had known the difficulties ahead?* The second person above added:

The initial warning signs made me want to help him. I managed to rationalize them, so I hadn't quite acknowledged the seriousness of his behaviors. If I had really thought about his behaviors, I wouldn't have entered into the relationship. However, picking up on and acknowledging the warning signs is much easier to do in hindsight.

Over the years, we have received the same type of feedback from men who became involved with borderline women. There just were not as many written comments from men to the survey.

Blind Spots Where Borderline HCPs Can Hide

As with the other high-conflict types, there are certain qualities of our own that can make us overlook the warning signs.

Low Self-Esteem

As the survey respondent said above, her partner "would warn me that he is not a very good person…" That can be very enticing for someone with low self-esteem. After all, if someone says that they are a lesser person than you, your self-esteem doesn't need to be threatened at all. This is someone you can feel okay with. Besides, they say that they *need you.* That in itself can make you feel better about yourself. If you can help them, you must be a good person, right?

Loved everything about me that made me insecure about myself.

Sure of himself, which gave me confidence.

Loneliness, Grief, Shyness

If you are lonely or grieving or shy, their charm and their desire to be with you may strike you as romantic, like the songs you heard growing up. *They need you!*—doesn't that sound sweet? It's just what you were looking for. Now you won't be alone anymore.

I was blinded by love, lust, and loneliness.

Naïve Beliefs

Isn't this love? Or are you mistaking warning signs for love? You'll recall that that's one of the naïve beliefs that can make us vulnerable to HCPs. But in reality, neediness and possessiveness are not romantic—they are signs of trouble.

Another naïve belief that can trip you up is the idea that you can change them. One of the most common blind spots when dating a borderline is wanting to help the person. Borderline HCPs often tell you that you make them a "whole person." Or they "can't live without you." They need you to "make them a better person." This pulls hard at our naïve beliefs.

I felt responsible for his feelings.

I thought perhaps he was just depressed and I could help him to see that he was a good person.

Time and love will not change them. *You* cannot change them. This is important to remember, because telling you that you can change them for the better is one of the most common ways that borderlines jam your radar. And if this reinforces your naïve belief that *you* can change them, don't believe it. No one can change another person. Only *they* can change themselves, and they usually aren't working on that. However, if they sincerely want to change, tell them to see a therapist. Those who really want to change will do that.

But most borderlines don't really want to change. They just want to be taken care of, the way a child is taken care of by an unconditionally caring parent. Hearing some of their backgrounds, you can understand why they would so desperately want something they never received. But you can't provide that for an adult and still hold onto yourself. A therapist can provide some of that unconditional acceptance (or, better yet, self-acceptance) in a well-structured therapy.

Quiz: Are You Dating a Borderline HCP?

Here's an informal quiz. It's not a scientific survey, but it can help you think about whether your partner might be a borderline HCP. You can also take this test online: www.dating-radar.com. Answer with a "1" for yes and "0" for no.

Your partner:

_____ Runs hot and cold, sort of a love you/hate you pattern.

_____ Targets and blames certain people close to you (sees them as threats) and tries to cut you off from some family and friends.

_____ Rages (screaming, yelling, hitting, biting, scratching, throwing, driving recklessly, destroying property).

_____ Needs to know where you are or be connected to you in some way most or all of the time.

_____ Can be truly empathic but then surprise attack on occasion.

_____ Constantly tests your love for them.

_____ Self-sabotages.

_____ Uses substances like alcohol or drugs to alleviate emotional pain or stress.

_____ Can't handle criticism (or most feedback) and seems overly sensitive.

_____ Hates being interrupted.

_____ Says things like, "I guess I'm just bad."

_____ Self-harms.

_____ TOTAL

0	Green (mild)	Take the test again or ask a trusted friend for input, to be sure you're not missing something. If you get 0 again, go for it—but keep your eyes open.
1 - 3	Yellow (spicy)	Consider getting out now. If you're not ready to get out, proceed with caution.
4 - 12	Red (nuclear)	Don't commit to this person unless you're ready to sacrifice.

Conclusion

Relationships with borderline HCPs can be fun, tantalizing, and intoxicating at first, but eventually the switch will be flipped and you will become the person's constant target of blame. Anyone who has experienced this type of relationship describes it as being in a deep, dark hole with no way to escape. The borderline HCP's predictable pattern of pulling you in then pushing you out, blaming you, yo-yoing back and forth, threatening suicide, being moody and depressed, and seeking revenge and vindication will unravel your confidence; harm or destroy relationships with your family, kids, and friends; land you in jail; or end your job. In the most extreme and rare cases, the combination of impulsiveness and rage of this personality type has resulted in injury or death.

Remember, they aren't bad people; they don't even know they operate this way. But by avoiding relationships with them, you not only protect yourself, you ultimately help the person by showing them that their behavior is not acceptable to you. You are not the one to help them, at least not until they've sought treatment. You likely won't give them insight, but your actions may be part of a string of events that eventually forces them into seeking professional help. A particularly good treatment method is DBT (dialectical behavior therapy), with many trained counselors available in many cities.

In terms of your dating radar, the most common warning signs are extreme mood swings, sudden and intense anger, and seeking revenge and vindication—over and over again. Unlike narcissistic HCPs, this pattern of behavior may not be obvious for months, and sometimes up to a year, especially if you don't know much about the person's history. Therefore, your radar may be easily jammed by extreme charm, offers of (or requests for) protectiveness, and apparent compatibility. Borderline HCPs can be particularly engaging and endearing. You need to be aware of this so you are not seduced into believing this is how it will always be.

If you have blind spots of low self-esteem, grieving, or shyness, a person with this personality type may really pull you in by emphasizing how extremely important and ideal you are to them. This can feel very reassuring, but it's really a trap that will flip against you suddenly. Watch out for expectations that time and love will change them, or that *you* can change them. You know by now that's not true.

CHAPTER SIX

Don't Be Seduced by a Sociopath!

"You will serve them; they will destroy you."

Core Fear – Being Dominated

Sociopaths (antisocials) require the strongest dating radar, because they are the best at deception. They will distract you and keep you from figuring them out, while at the same time charming the pants off of you (literally!). You often don't realize who you're dealing with until you've been totally taken advantage of and your life is ruins.

At the spicy-to-nuclear end of the continuum, these folks have what is known as antisocial personality disorder in the *DSM-5*. The terms *sociopath* and *antisocial* are fairly equivalent. Essentially, these people operate *against society*. They readily and frequently violate the law, as well as many of the unwritten rules for social relations, without remorse. Since these terms are fairly equivalent, we will use both in this chapter.

Sociopaths are always hustling to get whatever they want. They are constantly lying (even when you can catch them) and telling stories of how they have been taken advantage of. Yes!— They often succeed at making it seem that *they* are the ones who have been ripped off or victimized, when the truth is that *they* are the ones constantly ripping off and victimizing other people.

Conning is the word most often associated with sociopaths. Yes, many of them are criminals, although many have not yet been caught. They can drain your life savings and retirement plans along with your heart. They are users. They can con six people into marrying them and supporting them, all at the same time, hiding the existence of each from all the others. There have been entertaining stories of what happens when all the spouses get together and confront the con artist. Movies have been made on this premise.

In fact, there may be more movies about sociopaths than any other personality type, because they are so interesting as characters. Their charm and magnetism can't be matched. Yet they create extreme devastation in their victims' lives. Talk about plot! They steal from, humiliate, and lie to their romantic partners. But none of this is obvious at first. They are the absolute best not just at fooling their romantic partners—at fooling *everyone*.

The good news is that they generally don't stick around too long once you catch them in their lying, stealing, and cheating. Typically, they take off and start over with another relationship partner. But they will stick around as long as you serve their purposes. As long as they can keep you hooked into their worldview. As long as you're believing their lies, supporting their lifestyle, and bending to their will.

The prevalence of antisocial personality disorder is just under 4 percent of the population, according to the large NIH study (Grant et al. 2008). The vast majority are men (about three-quarters), but that still leaves a lot of antisocial women in the world. You have to be keenly aware and watch for signs in both men and women. And whatever your age, you need to beware of this personality almost more than all the others. They can do as much or more harm, and they are the best at fooling you.

Fear Factor: Being Dominated

The sociopathic HCP is driven by a fear of feeling dominated. Like other HCPs, their core fear drives them to con and manipulate you because of their never-ending need to be on top and dominate everyone around them. Antisocial personality disorder may be the most biologically-based personality disorder, as many people seem to just be born this way. It's as if they lack the basic wiring for connection, compassion, and cooperation. However, some experienced extreme abuse as children and they became cold and cunning out of necessity at the time. For the child, adopting those traits may have been a form of self-defense. In the hands of an adult, they become a weapon.

Sociopath HCP
FEAR OF BEING **DOMINATED**
Breaks rules & laws Deceptive Con artist
Needs to **dominate**

When do antisocial HCPs feel dominated?

1. When they feel that they don't have an advantage over you
2. When they feel that you're trying to control them
3. When they haven't conquered you
4. When you accuse them of lying or cheating
5. When you stop playing their games
6. When they have to comply with laws, rules, or policies
7. When they are questioned about anything

The moment any of these feelings of being dominated is triggered, they must do whatever it takes to feel dominating and in control again. They react with hostility, which ultimately sabotages the relationship. It's truly not optional for them. They're programmed this way, but they don't know it.

They are constantly gathering and assessing information for threats to their domination. They have to destroy the threat before it destroys them or interferes with their feeling of power and control. Like the other personalities, they don't think before pulling the trigger. They have to be mean, lie, manipulate, whatever it takes to feel on top again. Most people can be mean on occasion, tell a lie, or be manipulative; but for the average person it's not a compulsion as it is for the antisocial HCP. Whereas most people can regulate their impulses to be mean, lie, or manipulate, antisocial HCPs do not. They cannot tolerate feeling like they're not the ones in charge.

If you think that you wouldn't be stupid enough to be sucked in by someone like this, you're not alone in that belief. We like to think that sociopaths walk around with the sign of the devil on their foreheads, but they don't. We like to think they don't operate in our sphere, but they do.

They get married, just like anyone else. In some cases we know about, they were married for ten, twenty, even thirty years before their spouses had a clue that they were sociopaths and engaged in numerous misdeeds at work or in their communities—behind their spouses' backs.

It's not stupidity—it's called being conned. And it can happen to just about anyone. Men and women. Young and old. Rich and poor. But if you know what to look for, you'll be able to spot a lot of signs, even early on. Hone your dating radar, and catch these folks before they catch you!

30 Days with a Fighter Pilot

After a few weeks on Match.com, I met Kyle. He immediately stood out because his profile picture was turned sideways instead of vertically. Most guys I met online were eager to tell me everything about themselves—almost as if they were trying to sell a car. But Kyle was different. He didn't sell himself like the others did. In fact, he seemed reluctant to talk about himself or to interact much with me at all. In my mind, this made him stand out from the crowd and made me more curious to know him.

After a few messages back and forth, he started to act more interested and then began sharing more information. He was a fighter pilot in the military with the highest honors after several tours of duty in the Middle East and Eastern Europe. He was also a divorced dad with three kids and had coparented well with their mother. Now he was semiretired and working in a high-ranking capacity training future pilots and enjoying his favorite pastime—investing in the stock market.

Well, that was pretty exciting! A smart, well-established, stable guy who was interested in me of all people! He came across as a perfect gentleman and charming, but not in a smarmy way.

The long phone conversations commenced. Sparks flew! I was falling for this guy! I was giddy and thought of nothing but him every waking moment. After several long phone calls, he finally asked me on a date, and we met at an outdoor shopping mall. He treated me with kindness, opening doors for me, watching for branches above my head and uneven pavement beneath my feet. Within five minutes, we began kissing and didn't stop for what seemed like hours. I don't even remember if we went to dinner.

I was "in,"—hook, line, and sinker! He was good-looking, confident, successful, and totally in love with me. He told me he loved me within a week of that first date. Over the next thirty days, we went on dates and spent every available minute talking on the phone, emailing, texting, instant messaging. Every morning an email declaring his love and adoration awaited me. In HUGE font.

I felt loved, adored, almost worshipped. Most importantly, I felt protected. After a long line of loser dates, the stars aligned with this guy. Within a week we knew we were meant for each other and decided we would get married. We canceled our Match.com accounts and I let him meet my kids because it seemed so right. He even sat at the piano with my little girl while she showed off her piano playing ability. He took an interest in them and their well-being. Wow, I could breathe. This guy was amazing and my future was set.

We went on a drive one afternoon, parking at a beautiful spot overlooking a lake. He got quiet, turned to look me directly in the eyes, held my face gently in his hands, and said he could tell that I'd had some trauma in my background and asked if I'd like to share it with him. After promising complete confidentiality (actually telling me he was a "safe" person with whom I could trust this information), I opened my heart and my mouth, revealing my childhood sexual abuse. He made me look him in the eyes (his were moist with tears) as he promised to protect me every day that I walked this earth. He told me he was sorry for everything I'd been through, but I'd never have to worry about it ever again. He was there to protect me and my emotions.

What's not to love? To sink into? I felt loved, safe, and protected for the first time in my life.

On day 29, Kyle invited me to his home to spend the entire day with him. His home was pristine. Pictures of him in uniform standing by fighter jets lined the walls, alongside medals of honor. After a beautiful lunch that he'd lovingly prepared, he asked if I was comfortable moving to the bedroom. Of course I was comfortable! He was now my everything, and sealing the deal with the next step seemed entirely natural. He wanted to "show me" what it was like to be truly loved by a good person. We spent hours together in bed. He focused entirely on me and making me happy...for hours. At one point I began crying— the happy kind of crying. I remember my feeling so vividly that afternoon. I had met my knight in shining armor. All defenses were down.

The very next day he phoned to tell me his family had experienced a tragedy in another state on the other side of the country. Because he was the oldest of all the siblings, his presence and guidance were needed. I assumed he was going to fly there for a week or two. But no, he was moving there—immediately. And that meant that he had to break up with me.

My mind was reeling. I couldn't believe that he would even consider breaking it off. Distance didn't matter—love mattered. Of course we could make it work, even long distance. Why would he have to end things just because he was moving? It didn't make sense, but my brain still believed everything he'd promised in the preceding twenty-nine days, so I went into problem-solving mode. We can make this work! I could eventually move to join him there. But he kept saying it couldn't work. He had to end it and it was simply too painful to even see me again, so he had to just say goodbye.

I was utterly and completely shattered. I'd placed all my trust in him and put my heart and future right in his hands. Nothing up to this point even whispered that he was anything less than stable and honorable. But he was gone…just like that. My dreams, my future, simply vanished just as quickly as they'd arrived. I couldn't wrap my head around the reality that it was over, that we couldn't somehow make this work, that he wouldn't even discuss it with me.

After a few days of wallowing in my profound confusion, panic, and grief, I stepped outside to pick up the Saturday morning newspaper from the front porch. A front-page story reported that a fighter pilot had been dismissed from the military for violating a law against bringing strippers onto the military base. (Kyle had previously hinted that something big and important would be coming out about him. I'd assumed he was going to receive a Congressional Medal of Honor or something).

Still, I continued to believe his story about the family tragedy.

I never saw him again, but about a week after he broke up with me, a friend called to tell me that she'd come across a guy on Match.com whose picture was turned sideways. He was a fighter pilot and seemed reticent about offering more information about himself. She recalled my story and promptly blasted him.

He'd never moved. There was no family tragedy. My mind could not reconcile what had happened. How had I been fooled? How could I have been so blind? I blamed myself. What had I done to scare him away? Was I not pretty enough? It must have been something related to that afternoon in bed. What had I done?

It took several years and a few thousand dollars spent on therapy to see that my belief in Kyle was wishful thinking, to understand why I'd succumbed to it, and to explain to myself why it took this guy just 30 days to nearly destroy my life.

How did she miss the signs? Well, they were subtle in the beginning, making them harder to detect. The combination of her vulnerability from past trauma and moving too fast in the beginning of the relationship were a perfect setup—or rather, a perfect storm.

Four Months in the Spider's Web

I met my future wife in medical school. She was stunningly beautiful, extremely smart, personable, and funny. She liked to make everyone around her feel good and feel included. Even though I was kind of a shy guy, I was voted the Most Eligible Bachelor at our school the year I met her, so it wasn't like it was difficult for me to meet women. I'd dated a lot but I fell for her. There was something especially charming about her.

Medical school was difficult for me, but she sailed through it. She tried to encourage me but it didn't always feel genuine.

After finishing medical school, we both got jobs in another state. We moved there together, bought a house, and got engaged. We began building our careers and developing friendships at work and in the neighborhood. We had a great life together and she seemed to really have it together—even more than I did. I admired her ability to get along with everyone, work hard, excel in her medical practice…everything. She was on top of the world and everyone adored her.

A few things stood out as strange, but I wrote them off. The first was a phobia about sharp knives. Any time she saw a knife, she'd freeze and act completely terrified. She'd explained that when she was a child, one of her parents had kidnapped her and her siblings and held them hostage at knifepoint. It was an incredible story, but it made sense. Who wouldn't be terrified of knives after going through something like that?

The second was that she stated a desire for a small wedding and a plain wedding dress because, in her words, she wasn't comfortable with attention being focused on her. Oddly, she normally dressed seductively and didn't seem to have a problem being the center of attention in any setting. We ended up with 700 people at our wedding, and she wore a sparkling, glamorous, attention-getting dress. It was so confusing.

The third strange thing was her insistence that she was somewhat of a prude when, in reality, she was quite the opposite. Even in professional settings, she dressed in short skirts and low-cut blouses. She was extremely flirtatious but explained it away as friendliness, and would give me a quizzical, "are you nuts?" look when I brought it up.

There were some unusual incidents with other people, too. But I chalked them up to her friendliness. For example, she befriended a neighbor across the street, a man who lived alone and didn't seem to have many friends. She went out of her way to be neighborly, and made it a point to stop and chat with him whenever he was in his front yard. One day he left a note on our front door asking if she could stop by to help him with something. Her response was to call the cops and report him as a stalker! I was so confused. What was I missing?

Our life changed a lot after we got married. She was always going somewhere—had to work, had someone to meet, things to do. And she was so exhausted at night that she hardly ever wanted to do anything with me. I convinced myself it was normal post-wedding life.

Four months after the wedding I received a strange text from her that, as it turns out, wasn't intended for me. And it was accompanied by a picture of her naked breasts. I was shocked and didn't want to believe it.

Before approaching her, I decided to ask her closest friend about it. That opened the floodgates of information. She filled in the blanks that I didn't even know were there.

It turns out that my wife had been seeing other guys all along. Some were men from her past who would come to town and spend a night or two at a hotel with her. Matching up the dates, I realized those were explained away as nights when she was "on-call" at the hospital.

My wife's friend really spilled the beans. She told me that my wife had intentionally targeted the chief of staff in one hospital and the CFO in another hospital, drawing them into affairs with her. Both were married with young families. She had joked with her friend about drawing them into her "spider web" like a black widow. She tempted them with her charm, beauty, and subtle flirting until they took the bait. As soon as they started buying gifts and leaving notes for her, she reported them to the human resources department for harassment and stalking. Their careers and families were put in jeopardy. The friend reported that she herself had known both men for a long time and knew them to be good husbands who, to her knowledge, hadn't crossed that line with other women.

Even her friends weren't immune from being a target of the black widow. When this friend became suspicious and questioned my wife, she was accused of trying to harass her. The friend emailed a termination of friendship letter to her and pleaded with her to end the relationship with me before the wedding, before she destroyed me. Their friendship ended there.

We divorced shortly after. I didn't want to fight with her. I knew I wouldn't win. So I signed everything over to her. That was fine with her. I lost pretty much everything in a financial sense, but I was frightened and repulsed enough to know that fighting for anything wouldn't end well for me. She'd immediately begun threatening to destroy my career and my relationships with family and friends. With absolute calm and a sweet smile, looking me straight in the eyes, she promised to destroy me with ease because people would believe anything she said. She guaranteed that she could devise very creative stories about my past. These would go straight to my employer and the medical licensing and complaint board. My student loans were in the hundreds of thousands of dollars. Everything I'd worked toward for fifteen years was at stake.

She'd been done with me for a while, anyway. I realized that I'd loved her like a normal person loves someone, but she hadn't ever really loved me. As time passed, so did the confusion as I matched stories with reality and came to the realization that I'd been conned.

I asked her friend why she didn't warn me before the wedding. She said she was genuinely terrified of my fiancée, and she figured I wouldn't believe her. Ten years have passed since the divorce, and I continue hearing stories of her path of destruction from hospital to hospital in different states. Thank God I didn't have kids with her!

Note that in this situation, we don't know if her hostage at knifepoint story was true or not. She could have fabricated it for attention, or it could have been real, in which case extreme trauma could be part of what shaped her sociopathic future.

What's Special About Sociopaths

People with antisocial personalities want what they want, and they want it now. They are in many ways like three-year-olds, as they see a shiny object and want it desperately. They will then do whatever it takes to get the shiny object, without regard for the people they may hurt in the process. You would think that the thought of morality will cross their minds at some point, but it doesn't. What you think should be, isn't. Now, of course there is a wide range of severity of this pattern, so that you may see it occurring in very subtle ways in some cases.

One of the most common arenas for shenanigans is the financial world. People with antisocial personalities generally want money, so many of them are in business and some of them are on Wall Street, conning investors at all levels, from very small to very large. Others are embezzlers stealing money from their employers, most commonly small businesses or not-for-profit organizations like churches. They will use relationships to gain access to information or to other relationships that will advance their cause. In other words, they may be dating you solely because you (or your father or mother) have substantial assets, or access to other people's substantial assets.

But it's not just money they want. It's often power and control, and they'll do almost anything to get it. Sociopaths can insinuate themselves in academia or in the professions, where there may be many high-minded, big-hearted people who can be easily taken advantage of. Another obvious target is religious institutions. Worshipers are charmed and wooed by con artists because their big hearts and their faith—including perhaps a reliance on prayer or trust over reason—can create a blind spot. Regardless of the exact setting, what the sociopath wants may be a title or high position that allows them to manipulate and control a lot of other people. Their conscience doesn't affect them the way yours affects you.

In their romantic relationships, sociopaths love the challenge of wooing and landing a partner. It's hard to believe that people approach romance in such a calculated way, but they do. It's a mistake, though, to think that they'll always go for the best-looking or the richest partner. While that may be true in some cases, what they're really seeking is a relationship with someone who gives them an advantage or a connection, or gets their foot in the door. A sociopathic man may go for the best-looking woman because it makes him look good and gives him an advantage socially. Another sociopathic man may go for a not-so-attractive woman because she has a large bank account. One way or another, they use the partner to their advantage.

They seem to enjoy dominating others and do everything they can to avoid being dominated themselves. Often, their scheming is behind their partner's back. For many of them, their actions lead to legal trouble, so they get locked up for a while, where they are dominated by others (prison guards, more violent inmates, and so on). The majority are never locked up and some never do anything illegal—but they get very close to it, and those they take from feel seriously violated.

Since you'll definitely want to avoid sociopaths as partners, it helps to know what their relationships patterns are like. They spend most of their time hustling and conning to get what they want. In dating, this takes the form of love-bombing. Sociopaths can beat narcissists at charm, because they generally don't try to shift the focus to themselves. They really can stay focused on you and your interests and needs, until they've seduced you— that is, they've gotten you committed to the relationship. Then, they will either use you to advance their own schemes or get bored and move on to the next shiny object.

Key Characteristics

Here are common relationship issues we've noticed in sociopaths (or those with antisocial personality disorder) who are also HCPs. It should be noted that there are, in fact, some sociopaths who lack some of these characteristics. There are bank robbers and embezzlers, for example, who don't target individuals and aren't obviously cold and cruel.

As with all the other HCPs, they see the world in all-or-nothing terms. In this case: people are allies (partners in their schemes) or suckers—but usually not for long because they quickly move on to their next target after getting what they want.

1. They are constantly lying and deceiving others, including their relationship partners.
2. They use their relationship partners for status, for financial support, for making babies (although they don't take care of them), for a comfortable place to live, for their credit cards, and so on. They like the convenience of responsible spouses, who give them a good public image.
3. They are constantly telling compelling stories about how

they have been cheated, lied to, abused, treated unfairly, injured, and otherwise taken advantage of. They use these stories to get you to take care of them, lie for them to others, or give them your money.

4. They can be very cold and cruel in relationships. Domestic violence is common (although not universal). They often enjoy confronting and humiliating others, and they are more likely than the other high-conflict personalities to get into violent confrontations in public.

5. They are very impulsive, and they're big risk-takers. They seek the chemical rush of living life on the edge and challenging nature and other people in high-risk ways. Their risk-taking adventures can include their partners and their children, who are often terrified, but the sociopath doesn't care.

6. They can be very irresponsible. They don't like to work for other people, and some don't like to work at all. They generally don't want to do the work of raising children, although they often say the words that sound good.

7. Some of them have completely secret lives that their partners know nothing about. This can range from having secret affairs to illegal schemes (bank robberies, child pornography, and so on) to being a serial killer.

8. They often create a really good appearance to others, such as being active churchgoers, volunteering for good causes, and taking care of people in distress.

9. They are very aggressive in much of what they do, in their efforts to dominate others and take risks.

10. They truly lack empathy and remorse for their actions.

11. They really don't care about their partners, even though they say they do.

12. They're very sexual, although they're more excited by the conquest than by an ongoing intimate relationship.

Overall, there's a wide range of people with this personality pattern. Some are very dangerous, while others are just running minor schemes and may be mostly harmless to society. But even the less harmful ones don't make good relationship partners, because they are completely lacking in empathy, and they can't shift out of their scheming ways and share themselves at a deeper level. Their words can be very lovely and they can put on a good show for you. However, as partners, they are potentially devastating in both the short-term and the long-term.

Domestic Violence

Unfortunately, domestic violence is common for this personality, as it is for borderline personalities. However, the violence has different qualities in the two cases. Borderline HCPs have hot, reactive anger, while antisocial HCPs generally have cold, calculated anger. These antisocial HCPs may decide that they are going to get even with their partner for some minor or nonexistent offense, when the partner is least suspecting it. Their violence can be very brutal, causing broken bones or other serious injuries, and sometimes landing their partners in the hospital or the morgue. It can also come in the form of emotional abuse. Here's what some of our survey respondents said:

She disparaged me to others in public ways, in particular if it was someone close to me.

My relationship with this man was the most terrifying thing I've ever experienced.

As he told me after we broke up "I am highly creative at negative behaviors that I enjoy in a negative way." From morning to night, he was happiest when he had me so stressed that I was having panic attacks.

Physically abused me during my chemotherapy treatment for cancer. Blamed me! Made me feel like it was all my fault. Never apologized for anything, not even the horrible physical abuse.

He would stalk me at times, and also take my keys and wallet, I would become his prisoner at times. He would have sex with me when I didn't want him to, even during or after a severe beating. Once he had sex with me right after I'd come home from the hospital after major abdominal surgery, which ended up putting me back in the hospital. He would also record us having sex without me knowing.

We are contacted nearly every day by people in bad relationships or in the worst divorces and coparenting cases. They're all disasters, but there's a difference between "regular" disasters and the sociopath tsunami. People separating from or divorcing sociopaths live in terror, especially if they share children.

We'll get a call, for example, from a mom desperately wanting to know how to get the court to block her ex-husband from being alone with the kids. Not because he's a jerk or has been mean to the kids, but because her experience with him has taught her that he is actually capable of killing them in order to punish her.

Lying and Deception

They can be the most persuasive liars. Many partners we have spoken with say that they were shocked at discovering completely parallel lives. The particulars have included not going to work at all (even though they dressed up and left each morning with a briefcase), constant use of prostitutes or online paid phone sex, gambling, drug dealing, and stealing. They are very good at lying on the spot. They'll cover up almost any activity by using angry and blaming comments to throw their challengers off the trail.

I didn't recognize them as red flags at the time, but I caught him in lies and he convinced me that I didn't see what was in my own hand.

He was a master manipulator and liar. I had no idea anyone could lie constantly and about everything. Made me feel like I was nothing.

…they find victims because they are good at what they do. They are good at lying. They are good at being whatever they need to be to get what they want. It is lying without remorse, which ends up being good lying. If you like frogs they will tell you they love frogs. They will invent entire lifetimes, entire families, entire extensive lies because getting what they want is paramount. They will say they've fostered children, tell you they had careers they didn't have, tell you detailed stories (with tears in their eyes) about how their ex was so unkind to them. My ex once told me, "I always get what I want. I become what people like. I become whatever I need to be. Then when I'm done with them—well I don't really need people, ever."

The problem is they hide what they need to hide. He hid other children and other marriages, lied about school and his career.

Pathologic.

They are the most likely to be the "catfishers" discussed in chapter 3. Some catfishers do it just because they're lonely and can't get anyone interested in them. When they get in too far and are eventually found out, they express real remorse and don't do it again. Sociopathic catfishers, on the other hand, are driven by their personalities to do it because they *can.* Or perhaps it's done out of revenge. They don't feel bad afterward, and they don't apologize. They create fake profile after fake profile. Some with a lot of time on their hands have hundreds of fake profiles going at the same time.

It was harder to do this prior to the age of online dating; now it's the easiest thing in the world. Anyone can set up a fake profile in minutes—grab a picture of a gorgeous person, make up a name and a story, and voilà, an entirely fake identify is created. Interestingly, when confronted these people typically don't have much to say. It's as if they are just driven to be schemers and scammers by their personality. The issue's not the issue: the personality's the issue.

Criminal Activities

Sociopaths often have a criminal history or have done things that are illegal, even if they haven't been caught. It can be wise to run a criminal background check on anyone you are dating, because sociopaths are the ones who may have a criminal record but fail to mention it. Or, in many cases, they do mention their record, but minimize it or say they were falsely accused and convicted.

Also, many people with this personality seem to have a record of traffic violations and unpaid fines. This seems to be the type of behavior that they feel they can get away with, because it's relatively minor. But it's a good clue if you see a pattern of illegal driving behavior. Remember, sociopaths chafe at rules. In their mind, the laws don't apply to them.

He enjoyed confronting authorities.

...the need to "beat" the government on taxes; admission of tax fraud...

...kicking animals...

He would threaten me, threaten to kidnap our son or take full custody.

False Allegations

It is very common for antisocial HCPs to make up false allegations against others (it could be anyone) to distract people from what they are doing. Also, if they ever get caught for an illegal scheme, they usually blame it on someone else and may get reduced sentences by testifying against their partners in crime.

They can be very persuasive in convincing others that their partners are the guilty party and that they just went along. This can be especially worrisome when they publicly accuse their romantic partners of sexual abuse, or other false allegations. They demand loyalty from others, but show no loyalty themselves.

When I filed for an emergency protective order, he unleashed hell on me. Served me with divorce papers at my hearing. Typical false allegations, called child services, etc. The abuse continued financially and legally and increased after my son and I were granted a more permanent domestic violence order. He's since violated the order.

She threatened to make allegations of domestic violence against me.

He frequently complained that his staff was out to get him. He said it was because he wanted to change things, and they were so afraid of change, such sticks in the mud, that they couldn't handle anything new. And that they made up lies about him.

By the Numbers

In answer to the question:

Would you consider your partner (or former partner) to have traits of one of the following personality disorders?

Approximately 13 percent said antisocial personality and approximately 17 percent said a combination of antisocial and narcissistic personalities. So this personality type is less prevalent than borderline or narcissistic, but still a strong presence. There's a lot of overlap, and some of the comments reflected that.

It is a horrible experience living with a narcissistic/antisocial person.

I feel I wasted nineteen years of my life with a person I never really knew. He was like a complete stranger when we separated.

Be aware that when the relationship finishes, you will experience the divorce from hell. This person will play every dirty trick in the book to get what they want, which includes trying to destroy you, your career, your self-esteem, your relationship with your children. And even when it is over, you still have to deal with their behavior. They generally don't change, so you have to. The way you deal with them is to keep it businesslike. Don't get emotional and don't let them push your buttons. They will use your children to get to you, so get good professional advice on how to maintain a relationship with your children, as this is critical for your children's future.

The last comment was by a person who said that their partner was narcissistic and antisocial. This is a good description of what it's like getting out of such a relationship, especially when children are involved. Even though the majority of those with antisocial personalities are men, this was written by a man about a woman. We have seen many high-conflict divorce cases, some involving HCP men and some involving HCP women that fit this description.

One of the most shocking things for many people is how willing their former loved one is to try to humiliate them, hurt them, and destroy them—even in public. This purposeful behavior and lack of remorse is generally most characteristic of antisocial personality. Borderlines and narcissists also may do these things, but more often just in a reactive manner, as opposed to intentionally. Regardless of what kind of thinking is behind their efforts to make your life miserable, it's terrible when it happens.

How Antisocial HCPs Jam Your Radar

Radar-jamming is the focus of antisocial (or sociopathic) behavior. Sociopaths are always scheming and trying to appear to be something other than what they are. That's why they're so often called con artists. They're constantly trying to jam your radar. And they can be extremely good at it.

Charm

Let's start with charm. Sociopaths can be the most charming people in the world. They are so good that when you have doubts, they will notice and be able to talk you out of them. They'll get you to have more confidence in them than you have in yourself.

Many people have told us how their self-esteem went down and they really grew to doubt themselves when living with an antisocial person. Think back to the fighter pilot and black widow stories, and how they started with charm. Read them again and highlight or jot down anything that seems charming.

Here are some more comments from our survey:

Seemed to focus on my abilities and characteristics to make me seem so much more than I really was.

He was very charming and likable in the world.

Extremely attentive. Love-bombing was a big thing in the beginning. He literally told me, "You are so perfect. I am the luckiest man alive." On a daily basis.

Charm is very powerful, and in the hands of a sociopath it's a weapon. All the more reason to wait a year before making a commitment, so that you don't lose yourself and your radar during your dating relationship.

Fake Compatibility

Sociopaths are also skilled at fake compatibility. Because they are such schemers, they can construct paperwork and photos that make them appear to be someone completely different from who they are.

They're compatible with everyone, but it's fake. It's made up. They will say they're interested in purple pancakes if they know you're interested in purple pancakes, or they'll say they love kids when in actuality they don't like kids at all. They excel at fake suitability.

Overt Sexuality

Overt sexuality is a strong part of who they are. They are big on sexual conquests and may be seductive and charming, until you've had sex. Then some of them start losing interest. The fighter pilot's interest completely disappeared immediately after he'd made his sexual conquest. Then he threw her to the wind without a second thought. No remorse whatsoever. He was on to the next one (or more than one) within a week. And she was left with complete devastation.

Others stay interested until they have children, then they start looking elsewhere for sex and a new challenge. These are the people who may have more than one marriage going at a time. While this is mostly a male thing, we have heard of women who have had several husbands at the same time—none of whom knew about the others, until they eventually did.

In the other situation, the self-described black widow was flirtatious and dressed provocatively while claiming to be the opposite. She was sleeping with several people at the same time while either engaged or married. She was beautiful, sexy, and smart, and she used those qualities to seduce and dominate. Men were willing to risk losing their careers and families for her. This is the kind of charm that's so powerful it can jam your radar.

Sex with a sociopath may be exciting initially, but later it leaves you with a disconnected, empty feeling because it's purely one-sided. After an initial "focused on you" phase, which you mistake for romance and altruism, the antisocial HCP becomes disconnected and focused on their own pleasure.

Fake Protectiveness

Fake protectiveness is very common with antisocial HCPs.

The fighter pilot used this tactic to bait the hook. As a victim of child sexual abuse, his girlfriend longed for someone protective, even if she didn't know it at the time. He used it to get what he wanted—sexual conquest.

A sociopath may even get into physical fights on your behalf. "I'm not going to let them talk to you that way! You've got it coming, buddy!" This is what you see a lot in the movies (especially old westerns). But there are people like this in real life. The trouble is that they could eventually turn on *you* and start beating *you* up. If you see a pattern of violence directed at others, you can expect that someday it will be directed at you. Sociopaths come across as protectors, promising, "No one is going to beat up on my wife." But in reality, they mean, "I'm the only one allowed to beat her."

Putting all of this together, you have to look closely at whether your dating partner engages in any of these radar-jamming behaviors. Are they "too good to be true?" Are they "amazingly compatible?" See how their interest holds up if you delay having sex. And don't get hooked into the romantic fantasies of the "protective" partner. These four areas of radar jamming really fit the common seductive behavior of antisocial personalities. If they're working too hard at these, be suspicious.

Blind Spots Where Sociopaths Can Hide

Antisocial HCPs are the most skilled at finding your blind spots and exploiting them. Any vulnerability is game for them. So it helps to be really aware of your own vulnerabilities and not let them be exploited.

Self-Esteem, Trauma, Abuse

Low self-esteem is like a magnet for sociopaths. They often play up how wonderful you are at the beginning, but then they'll turn on you, and say and do the cruelest things. So be careful about sharing your inner secrets too quickly with someone who seems to be pushing for your self-disclosure. The fighter pilot could have won an Oscar for his performance. He set the scene by taking her to a romantic, secluded spot. He looked deep in her eyes, holding her face intimately in his hands and telling her he knew she'd suffered in the past. She had no love for herself but this guy did, didn't he? So she told her most private secret… to a sociopath who would in short order drive her self-esteem and her trust in men even lower.

Sociopaths may tell you stories about having been victimized themselves, as part of their strategy to prey on you. So keep in mind that their own self-disclosure may be totally false, designed just to get you to open up.

A history of childhood abuse or trauma can make you especially vulnerable to antisocial HCPs. It's almost as if they have a sixth sense for finding people from vulnerable backgrounds.

The love-bombing was so intense, and coming from my background (rejection from mother, absent father, failed relationships) I know I would have ignored any red flags (and did!) for that level of attention and love.

Although I didn't know it at the time, my childhood abuse made me a perfect target for anyone, especially an antisocial. My self-esteem was in the toilet.

Loneliness, Grief, Shyness

If you are lonely or grieving or shy, you are an appealing target for conquest by a sociopath.

I'd known him for a few years but we went out for the first time one month before my father died. Then he moved in on me.

I was lonely.

They always try to isolate people so that they can feel in control. If you're already isolated by your loneliness, grief, or shyness, bonus! Part of the work is already done for them. This is a good reason to have other people with you when starting out dating someone.

While antisocial HCPs lack real empathy, they know that it's expected in relationships, and they are perfectly capable of faking it. So you have to be especially cautious. They may inundate you with sympathy and soothing promises. They may also shower you with more superficial (but still appealing) pleasures like gifts, compliments, and weekend getaways, but these things are meant to serve their purpose. They don't do things out of the goodness of their hearts. They don't have real empathy for you. Consider that whatever they say or do, the opposite may actually be actually true.

And however empathetic they might seem when they're preying on your vulnerability to reel you in, they eventually show their true sociopathic nature. Our survey respondents told us:

The first indication was that once when I was very upset about a disagreement we had, I started to cry. The crying did not elicit a sympathetic response or soften his heart; rather it angered and hardened him.

I got injured, and he showed no empathy. He laughed and told me to rub dirt in the wound.

Naïve beliefs

There are two naïve beliefs that can make you especially blind to antisocial HCPs. The first is the notion that getting serious very quickly is a sign that the relationship is "right" or meant to be. Antisocial HCPs want to move in on you really fast. Of all the HCP types, they are probably the most eager to start living together or get married.

Quick to get engaged. Had me wanting to buy a wedding dress before he even proposed. (I actually did.)

He said he wanted to marry me on our first date.

The fighter pilot started talking marriage before the two even met in person.

It's easy to interpret this rush to the altar as an indication of true and deep love, when in fact it is the opposite. It is calculated pressure. Remember, antisocial HCPs want what they want and they want it now. Relationships are mostly a tool for getting what they want. Don't be fooled by mistaking this warning sign for love.

And it is indeed a warning sign! Once you've made a commitment, the relationship can make an instant U-turn. After you're married, the antisocial may stop working or start using your credit card, or engage in any of a number of other take-advantage-of-you behaviors. They may turn on you like a vicious dog within hours or days. They may inform you that you're the biggest whore in the world. They may take control over you. You will become their property—theirs to do whatever they want with.

Borderlines may also want to move along quickly in

relationships, but for them it's more about needing to feel attached than about taking advantage or owning you, as it is for antisocial HCPs. There's no doubt about it: a romance with an antisocial is a match made in hell.

The second naïve belief that can make you vulnerable to a sociopath is the idea that you can change them. Sociopaths are also similar to borderlines in telling you how much you are helping them become a better person, and that they can't live without you. And they do need you to make them better—but only in the sense of improving their status.

Remember: Time and love will not change them. *You* cannot change them.

However, getting you to think you can change them for the better is one of the most common ways that antisocial HCPs get past your blind spots. This is especially common after you have found out about some of their very negative past behavior. They keep you in the relationship by promising to change, and they may actually act different for a while. But don't believe it. What you see now is what you will get more of in the future.

> *Took twenty years to realize that regardless of how hard I tried and the sacrifices I made, this would never change. And it took years of individual therapy to realize that I didn't deserve to be treated the way he treated me.*

> *I'm not sure he changed; it was just that life moved and he didn't, so things that I expected to change when we had jobs or a family, didn't. His own needs were always imperative.*

> *Recognize that you can't "fix" anyone but you!*

> *It feels like he has stolen my whole life and I cannot live a life in harmony with him around, especially because we have children.*

When I left him I had become "a shadow of my former self,"
always worried, scared, and insecure. It was an awful mess.

Remember that antisocial personality disorder may be
the most biological, born-this-way personality disorder. The
likelihood that an antisocial HCP will change is close to zero.
Don't be blind to this reality.

Quiz: Are You Dating a Sociopath?

Here's an informal quiz. It's not a scientific survey, but it
can help you think about whether your partner might be an
antisocial/sociopathic HCP. You can also take this test online:
www.dating-radar.com.

Answer with a "1" for yes and "0" for no.

Your partner:

_____ Breaks rules or laws casually; has a criminal
record or a lot of traffic violations.

_____ Is exceedingly charming or helpful in the
beginning.

_____ Steals or takes money from you; uses your credit
cards.

_____ Doesn't show real remorse.

_____ Is verbally or physically abusive or manipulative
when they feel dominated; is threatening or
violent in public (with you or others).

_____ Lies about almost everything; lies to manipulate
your emotions or to get your money.

_____ Has to be in control and make the rules. (You
have to ask permission or be "allowed" to go
places, talk to people, etc.)

_____ Never apologies, unless it's to get something they want.

_____ Doesn't respect your privacy or your dignity.

_____ Sabotages positive attention paid to you, or sabotages your events; punishes you later.

_____ Makes you feel confused about details that don't add up, like what they're doing, where they're going, who they're seeing.

_____ Cuts you off from family and friends.

_____ TOTAL

0	Green (mild)	Take the test again or ask a trusted friend for input, to be sure you're not missing something. If you get 0 again, go for it— but keep your eyes open.
1	Yellow (spicy)	Consider getting out now. If you're not ready to get out, proceed with caution.
2 - 12	Red (nuclear)	Don't commit to this person unless you're ready to sacrifice.

Conclusion

You wouldn't wish a romantic relationship with an antisocial HCP on your worst enemy. Time spent in relationships with antisocial HCPs can destroy your soul. They excel at making you think everything is your fault or that you're crazy. They do whatever it takes to feel dominant and in charge. Both men and women who have been in relationships with antisocial HCPs often spend years in therapy, engage in self-harming behaviors like drinking and drugs, end up depressed, and many vow to never marry again.

Your health, your finances, your reputation, your relationships—just about everything is at risk. In their world, nothing is beyond the pale. Sociopaths have been known to use their spouse's credit card to buy flowers for someone else they are dating. It's more than shocking; it's like being caught in a riptide in the ocean, because it's so contrary to your expectations of and experiences with fellow human beings.

This personality type may be the hardest for your radar to detect, so don't miss the subtle, seemingly small cues they'll give you. Make no mistake: they have a plan, and they're going to conquer you. If you don't stay alert to the red flags, you are at risk of losing your confidence in yourself and your decisions, and worst of all, you could lose your life. Your radar needs to be on high alert.

In summary, the warning signs include conning, lying, and willingness to hurt people without remorse. When you see these behaviors in how they treat other people, expect that it will eventually be how they treat you. It can take months or a year—or even more—to see these warning signs, because they cover them up so well.

A sociopath will work hard at jamming your radar. Charm to the max. Fake protectiveness is very common, especially if they are successful financially (legally or not). They may seem to want you to take care of them, if they think that will float your boat. And they are experts at fake compatibility, because they know how to create a fake history and they have the confidence to tell stories about shared interests that sound realistic.

They also work hard at making you doubt yourself. Sociopaths know your weaknesses, or they will quickly find them. Low self-esteem, loneliness, grieving, and shyness are their specialties. If you have these blind spots, learn how to watch out for those who will manipulate them. They will find your naïve beliefs and manipulate those as well, such as by telling you stories of how they've been a victim and need your help, and then they'll change. Trust us: they're lying to you.

CHAPTER SEVEN

Don't Hook Up with a Histrionic!

"You will give them all of your attention;
they'll give you none of theirs."

Core Fear – Being Ignored

People with histrionic personalities are, by definition, extremely dramatic. And, like thespians everywhere, they don't feel complete without an audience. Histrionic HCPs have a strong drive to be the center of attention. They love to tell tales of all the unbelievable experiences they've had—many of them about terrible things that have happened or that they fear will happen. Some of the stories are great exaggerations; others are outright fabrications. But their sagas are usually compelling, and it's hard to ignore them.

Just wait until they start telling stories about you. *Why would they do that?* you wonder. *I'm not that exciting.* Well, HCPs always look for a target of blame; that's what makes them high-conflict. And if you get involved with a histrionic HCP, you will—at some point—become their next target. You'll be the villain in their new thriller.

It's easy to get hooked, especially if you're a natural helper or fixer. Histrionic HCPs can be very exciting. They can sweep you off your feet with drama. Early on, someone else is the villain, and you'll feel like you really want to come to their aid—after "all they've been through." Often, the drama pulls at our heartstrings and we swoop in to save them, but then the help is rejected or not followed through.

While the excitement can be very seductive, the accuracy or severity of what they are telling you is often doubtful. Eventually you'll wear yourself out listening and helping, because if you don't put a stop to it or curb it, you'll have a new full-time job and no time for your life.

Gross exaggeration and outright lying comes naturally for people with histrionic personalities because they're driven by the need to be in the middle of everything. Exaggerating, or bending the truth is automatic—it gets them the attention they need and are desperate for. It's like oxygen to them.

The more extreme cases of this dramatic behavior rise to the level of pathology—in this case, histrionic personality disorder. This disorder is present in just under 2 percent of the general population, according to the large NIH study (Grant et al. 2008). While this emotion-based behavior has been traditionally associated with women, this study found that there are just as many men who display this disorder.

In reality, even though there is a small percentage of people with histrionic personality disorder, many more people have some histrionic traits. Slightly more than 8 percent of our survey respondents indicated that their high-conflict partner was the histrionic type. This number may be a false low because little is known by the general public about histrionic personalities, and many of the associated behaviors are incorrectly identified as borderline personalities.

Distinguishing between histrionic and borderline personalities can sometimes be confusing because both types tend to need to be the center of attention, and both can produce a lot of emotional drama. (And all four of the high-conflict personality types can be very overtly sexual.) The borderline personality pulls you in, pushes you away, gets angry and vengeful, but then pulls you back in again. The histrionic personality pulls you in and tries to keep you with them, to hear their stories until you're exhausted. They have a very hard time letting go of your attention.

Unlike borderline HCPs, histrionic HCPs generally don't get directly angry or sexually rejecting of you if they're upset. Instead, they just tell other people stories about you that make them look like a victim to get sympathy—and make you look like a terrible person. Ultimately, knowing specifically which personality type you're dealing with isn't as important as being aware of all of these patterns of behavior and cautious with all of them.

Many people with one of the other personality disorders also have traits of this disorder, so that there is a lot of drama surrounding them and their friendships and other relationships. It's easy to believe that they are intentionally stirring things up, but most of the time they are just being the way they are without even realizing it. They are constantly feeling triggered by outside events and they react to them with more intensity than most other people do.

Fear Factor: Being Ignored

The histrionic HCP is driven by a fear of feeling ignored. This fear often dates back to insecure attachments in early childhood, when they may have perceived that parents or other caregivers weren't really there for them. They seem to have a deep-seated sense of helplessness that drives them to create drama-filled crises on a consistent basis. They need people to like them and to pay attention to them, and they'll do just about anything to accomplish both.

Histrionic HCP
FEAR OF BEING **IGNORED**
Superficial & helpless Attention-seeking Exaggerates
Needs to be **center of attention**

When do they feel ignored or worried they won't be the center of attention?

1. Any time you're not looking at them or listening to them
2. When other people are getting the attention
3. When their own emotions feel overwhelming
4. When they get caught lying
5. When they think you don't see them as a victim
6. When you stop paying attention to their drama
7. When you don't buy into their stories

The moment they feel ignored or not involved in the conversation, they must do whatever it takes to feel that you're paying attention. Just like the other HCP personalities, their strategy is the opposite of what you'd expect. Instead of being aware that they're driving you crazy with their endless stories and drama, they're completely oblivious to it. They often react to being ignored by pouting, whining, using sexuality to lure you, or pouring on more drama. It's not optional for them. They're programmed this way, but most of them don't know it. If they're rejected, then they quickly tell their stories about you to as many other people as possible with as much drama as possible. And you may be shocked to find that many people take the histrionic

HCP's side after hearing their stories about you.

Just as with other HCPs, the histrionic brain is constantly gathering and assessing information for threats to their need for attention. Being ignored or left out feels unnatural and uncomfortable. It actually puts them in a fear state, which can be conquered only by doing something—anything—to grab your attention again.

"Secret" Weapon

Liam and I met in college, got married, and had five kids in eight years. Our relationship was very sexual from the beginning. I stayed in the background mostly, because everywhere we went he had to be the center of attention. He was extremely good-looking (tall, rugged, and muscular, with dark, curly hair) so I told myself that all the attention he got from women was due to his looks and the fact that he was very engaging and could hold an audience with his storytelling. He was also the biggest flirt in the world. A deadly combo: a handsome flirt.

We constantly lived on the edge financially because he job-hopped as a way of life. He always had a story about having been victimized by a former employer or coworkers. Once he started down this trail, it was paired with the next incredibly exciting opportunity awaiting him at the next place of employment. This went on the entire twenty-nine years we were married. We lost a house that had been given to us and we always had to drive broken-down cars. It was always a struggle.

After Liam's first few affairs, I distanced myself emotionally and held it together until the kids were off to college. The affairs never lasted long. Some of the women were people I knew, which was mortifying. A couple of them told me later that he'd told them lots of stuff about me, including very private, personal information. Then I filed for divorce and had him served with the papers. I had a feeling it wouldn't go well. I could have prepared him ahead of time but I suppose I was hoping to avoid a confrontation.

How I wish I'd have handled it differently to avoid his next actions. He came to my friend's house where I was staying temporarily and screamed at me that he was going to tell my secret to my entire family! This was a secret that I'd told no one but him—ever. Now he was going to reveal to my parents, siblings, and, the worst, my kids, that one of my brothers had sexually abused me during our childhood. To say his threat had a chilling effect on me is an understatement. Dread for what I had to do next would be more accurate.

One by one I told my secret to my kids and the rest of my family so they wouldn't have to hear it from him. My kids were furious. My parents didn't believe it. My siblings did, and cut our brother out of their lives. Now the family is in disarray. Only later did I find out that my oldest son had gone to his dad with a gun, threatening to blow his head off if he uttered a word to anyone. He never did.

How Fast Can You Go?

I met a girl on a two-hour flight. She was attractive, dressed professionally, and drew me in right away with her engrossing stories and brilliant conversation. She had bright blonde hair and a smile as big as Texas. I was smitten, kind of stumbling over myself and, yes, nearly drooling.

After a couple of drinks, her stories got louder and more detailed.

Wild stories about a lot of things, but mostly about her raucous sex life. She told me about a series of guys who had broken her heart. They were idiots, she said, and I agreed.

After another couple of drinks, her skirt was inching up and her hand was resting (well, sort of) on my leg. She jokingly asked if I wanted to join the "mile high club" with her. The flight landed soon thereafter and we walked off the plane, straight to a taxi, and off to a hotel. And thus began a fascinating love fest that lasted just a few short months. I was falling in love and wanted to marry her. She was pushing for an engagement ring within the first month. Girls didn't usually come on to me. They usually aren't into science guys, but she was the one who was.

So I bought a ring and proposed, and wedding preparations began. She controlled every aspect of the planning, and I just let her. The closer we got to the wedding, the more distant and colder she became. I thought it was pre-wedding jitters. The wedding day came and went matter-of-factly. Just one month later, I woke up to a note that said she'd made a mistake and had found that she couldn't live with a man who was so boring and lifeless. She'd met someone new and would be sending divorce papers soon.

In both of these stories, you see how the power of the drama and the excitement of their immediate sexual attraction clouded their thinking. Yet it wasn't just an exciting night together. In both cases, they moved right on into marriage, with the highest expectations. In the first case, by the time the problems became obvious they already had kids, so she stayed. It's no surprise that when she filed for divorce his reaction was a very dramatic one— to reveal her most personal secret and create chaos in her family. In the other story, it's no surprise that this exciting, dramatic woman found her new husband unappealing in the routines of married life. People with this personality often need new drama every day and quickly get bored. The way it started for him is probably the way it started for her with a lot of men. It's easy to confuse histrionic personalities for wonderful relationship potential."

What's Special About Histrionic HCPs?

People with histrionic personality disorder or traits can be engaging to the point of riveting. They are master storytellers. But when they feel threatened about the relationship (or bored and looking for excitement), they can also turn you into a target of blame and tell dramatic stories about you to embarrass and publicly humiliate you. They are emotionally reactive, seemingly driven by their own inner weather. Yet these emotions are superficial and fleeting.

As coworkers, they can be a big drag on productivity. It's hard to get much work done when they're around because they usually want to talk and talk before getting down to business. Whatever your relationship to them, if you're a person who likes to give people respect by listening, then pull up a chair, because you'll be listening for a long time. Boundaries are a must! Otherwise, you will become their favorite audience, and you'll hear every story and every variation of every story about themselves, their relationships, their neighbors, what they ate for lunch, their medical issue of the day. Everything is a story.

Drama rules their lives. In fact, they're lost without it. "You'll never believe what happened on my way to dinner!" "Wait 'til you hear what so-and-so did!" "I need to share something with you that's just absolutely horrifically emotionally devastating me." One of the quickest ways to spot this type is by their overexaggerated responses when you bring up a subject. The histrionic personality will respond to a minor statement with a huge response, like "Oh, my *God!*" or "Are you *serious?*" or "*What!?!?!?!*"

Once the histrionic HCP has pulled you into their orbit, you yourself will be the subject of many of the tales. They find it extraordinarily easy to talk about you to everyone you know. They don't keep confidences and are comfortable telling many others about your weaknesses and secrets. It's how they operate, but they're not really doing it on purpose. It's just how they developed. They're good at getting you to open up to them about your secrets. They may seem to be paying intent, rapt attention to your problem and expressing sincere concern, and so you may be tempted to divulge. They swear they won't tell anyone, but you'll later discover that just isn't true. Your information will be told "secretly" to everyone you know. So if there's any chance you might be dealing with a histrionic, it's a good idea to keep your secrets to yourself!

When you first get together with someone like this, they may shower you with attention. But look out, because it won't be long before indifference sets in. The excitement of a new relationship will disappear along with their attraction and commitment to you. They must have continual excitement in order to keep their fear of feeling ignored at bay. Before you know it, indifference shifts to abandonment of the relationship. Yes, the breakup will hit you out of nowhere. You may think that your relationship struggles are normal. All relationships can get a little boring and stale, but that's just a part of life, right? So you'll be surprised when your histrionic partner doesn't have the same perspective about that "part of life." They need to move on to the next person to refuel with excitement.

> *I wonder how she sleeps at night, knowing she's destroyed so many lives. Then I remind myself that she doesn't think about what she's done to past boyfriends because she's busy getting her next attention fix.*

> *...always got bored if things did not stay exciting, so this person changed their interests, partners, etc., often.*

Key Characteristics

Here's what you can expect if you're in a relationship with a histrionic HCP—whether they have the disorder or just traits.

1. They tell emotionally intense and compelling stories, often about terrible things that have happened to them or someone they know. They typically do this in a secretive, "you're the only one I'm telling" way.

2. They have a preoccupation with feeling helpless or victimized. They often blame others for how upset they feel, and see others as taking advantage of them. That may energize you to help them, but you'll only be met with another problem later, and another.

3. They often will bend your ear and prevent you from talking, or from ending the conversation.

4. They can be very sexually seductive, often in an exaggerated manner. In fact, this is typically one of the first signs you'll notice.

5. They can be provocative, by dressing suggestively or saying or doing things seemingly just to get a rise out of other people.

6. They believe their relationships are deeper than they

are, and that certain people care about them a lot more than they really do. They are easily disappointed. On the other hand, they can be skittish about committing to relationships as well. When they talk about a relationship or friendship, expect them to exaggerate the intimacy of it.

7. They can be very quick to divulge things publicly and share information without the normal boundaries—including intimate secrets they have been told by friends, relatives, or dating partners. They feed and enhance rumors on a regular basis. After they're long gone from your life, your friends will fill you in on your own secrets.

8. They tend to exaggerate facts or totally make up stories about things that have happened to them or people they know, and the stories often come with tears. The fabrication isn't done in a calculating way; it just comes naturally to them. They don't have filters for veracity of information, just as they have no filters for quantity of information.

9. They sometimes seem to feel like pincushions, so that everything registers as a pinprick or a stab in the back. They are constantly feeling caught by surprise when things turn out different from what they expected. You could say they're overly sensitive.

10. They can be very dependent on their dating partners and spouses and even children. They like to be taken care of. It's rarely done correctly in their eyes, though; you can never give enough to satisfy their needs.

11. They may complain a lot about physical ailments and spend more time than average with doctors and other

healthcare professionals. This a classic, telltale sign.

12. If there is a breakup, they may reveal or threaten to reveal their partner's most intimate secrets and become preoccupied with publicly blaming and shaming their former partner.

As with the other high-conflict personalities, there's a wide range of severity of these problems. Some are mild. These are the folks who just go on too long about their own problems and don't seem to recognize when you're trying (politely) to bring the conversation to a close. Others are downright nuclear. These are the ones who think, write, speak, and act in all-caps, no matter what the topic. No gesture is too grand. They leave a trail of dramatic devastation behind them wherever they go.

In contrast to the other personalities discussed so far, histrionic HCPs tend to show you who they are right from the beginning. There is always a recognizable element of heightened emotions and drama. So you are less likely to be totally caught by surprise later on. On the other hand, these qualities can be very appealing and seductive, so that people sometimes miss the warning signs. Some come across as very real, genuine, and down-to-earth. You may also be attracted to the immediate intimacy they offer. It's easy to feel comfortable with them right away, because they are so good at connecting.

False Public Allegations

The main extra problem that seems associated with histrionic personalities is their tendency to make false allegations and to spread rumors widely. It's not always clear whether they believe the stories they make up, or if they know they're made up. The accusations and rumormongering are most likely to occur after a breakup, but in some cases occur throughout the relationship. People with this personality often tell the world that they played a much bigger, positive role in the relationship, while the other person was a terrible or irresponsible partner.

> *She once told me that lying was a part of her, so much so that she truly believed the lies she told. Catching her in a lie was impossible.*

One wonders whether this personality style explains the judge's opinion we referred to in chapter 3, regarding the divorce of Paul McCartney and Heather Mills:

> *I wholly reject her account that she rekindled the husband's professional flame and gave him back his confidence. I have to say that the wife's evidence that in some way she was the husband's "psychologist," even allowing for hyperbole, is typical of her make-belief. (Gammell and Rayner 2008)*

Bill remembers one particular case he had in court. He represented the husband, and the wife had at least histrionic traits, if not histrionic personality disorder. She was caught making up a story during a court hearing, which was easily disproved. But then she burst into tears and insisted that she believed the story. The judge seemed to buy it, and she never experienced consequences for fabricating those events.

Histrionic personalities often use tears in the courtroom. In fact, you can expect tears any time they're questioned. It goes with the territory. They may be very likeable and able to get you to listen, but once you question them about the accuracy of their claims, they will usually immediately go into victim mode and then here come the tears. Again, they don't try to be this way—it's their operating system.

It's a powerful thing, when you are on the wrong side of a histrionic HCP in public. The histrionic HCP is often believed over the innocent person (their target of blame) because of the intensity of their emotions. It's easy to get things backward due to this intensity. Our brains are wired to pay attention to drama and our natural instinct may be to empathize with and protect the "victim." This seems to be because most people empathize with their distress to some extent, and mistakenly believe there must be some truth to their complaint. "What did you do to make her (him) so upset?" people often ask. What they don't realize is that people with personality disorders can make up stories with absolutely no basis in reality—but they sound and feel true, even to the person who's telling them. "Emotional facts" is what we call this phenomenon.

By the Numbers

Slightly more than 10 percent of survey respondents listed histrionic traits in response to the following question:

Would you consider your partner (or former partner) to have traits of one of the following personality disorders?

In terms of warning signs, here's what a few people said:

Moodiness. Unsure about my feelings about her. Big reactions to small things.

Excessive jealousy, overly emotional reactions, rushing the pace of the relationship, dramatic overtures. Examples: interfered with friendships with other males, threats of physical violence against romantic rivals, insisting we were "soul mates" and "meant to be together," showering with excessive compliments like "You are the sexiest and most beautiful woman in the whole world and I can't live without you." One time early on, during an argument, he put a knife to his own throat and said, "I would rather die than live without you."

He would react very emotionally and with very juvenile reactions to frustrating situations. For instance, when he was struggling financially he literally threw a fit and pouted when he saw a jacket that he couldn't afford.

The relationship wasn't too bad while I was agreeable to what he wanted and thought he was wonderful. It was so easy for me to "understand" why he reacted the way he did. He was always suffering in some way—not getting along with others, so many pressures on him, his family was highly critical, etc.

Note the phrases like "big reactions to small things," "dramatic overtures," "threw a fit," "always suffering," and "so many pressures." If those words seem familiar, you may be dealing with a histrionic HCP.

How Histrionic HCPs Jam Your Radar

Compared to the other high-conflict personalities, histrionic HCPs don't put as much effort into deception. Instead, the problem is that they are so dramatic and emotional that you are distracted from the reality of the situation. It takes longer to sort through the drama to get to the bottom of things—the real story. Sometimes some of it is true but it will take you a long time listening to it, sorting through it, and finding evidence to support it. All of the drama and exhausting listening can keep you too busy to notice that it's not a healthy relationship.

Charm

Yes, they can be very charming. But the behavior is often so over the top that it is annoying or silly, rather than romantic. For example, consider the man who, early in the relationship, held a knife to his throat to show his love for his partner. He was also in the habit of giving her "excessive compliments." Maybe she actually found that charming—or maybe she simply overlooked it in hopes that the relationship would work out.

You'll feel more flattered by histrionic HCPs than you'll feel when given compliments by the average person. Their praise is very intentional and intensely focused on you. We all like compliments, but if you feel the flattery is excessive, it may be a warning sign.

Along with the charm may come gifts, cards, and offers of help. These may be nice, but they're also possible red flags. The sentiment may be genuine, but think about the central fear driving this personality. More than anything, they are allergic to being ignored. Does the constant charm or gift-giving draw attention to them?

> *He was always showering me with praise and compliments, which was nice in the beginning, but right after a compliment came a shift of attention back to him. I thought he was listening, but it felt fake.*

They may charm you at first by idealizing you, but look out, because it won't last. Before long, they'll get bored and move on to someone new.

Fake Compatibility

Although fake compatibility is a hallmark of most HCPs, as

illustrated in previous chapters, it was hardly mentioned in the comments from survey respondents about the histrionic personality. Perhaps that's because these dramatic personalities ("dramatics") aren't very good at faking things—they are too busy overreacting to things. But we're sure that some dramatics can imply compatibility to some extent, especially if they also have one of the other high-conflict personalities.

If you're not sure whether you're dealing with fake compatibility, think back to the core fear: feeling ignored. They may overstate compatibility with you in order to get your attention, but it's the exaggeration, not the fake compatibility, that pegs them as a histrionic.

Overt Sexuality

Intense, expressive sexuality is a big part of this highly emotional personality. This can be so exciting and potentially satisfying that it can cover up all the other drama and emotional extremes—at least for a while. One comment referred to this with an apparently histrionic man:

Wanted sex multiple times a day. Eventually, I told him I felt he was using me and he said, "I just am so turned on to you."

Pretty much anyone, no matter how unattractive or different in age, who approached her in a bar, would be treated to extensive flirting.

There are men she'd meet and sleep with all in the same night—mostly my husband's friends; then she'd try to pressure them into relationships.

...she often makes inappropriate and outrageous physical contact with me.

People with histrionic personalities aren't necessarily out to lure you into relationships, although you'll think they are. It is difficult to wrap your head around the idea that they don't set out intentionally to flirt with you when they easily end up having sex with you. They seduce without even realizing they're doing it. It's just their natural way of interacting with people. What they see as innocent, friendly conversation is viewed by objective observers as overtly sexual and flirtatious. They have a hard time keeping friends of the same sex (particularly women) because their friends get tired of them flirting with their husbands. They're stunned to learn that their friends have forbidden their husbands from talking to them, whether they would actually sleep with a married man or not.

They're often accused of leading people on, teasing them with the possibility of sex. In some instances, they are. But again, because this is their internal operating system—they may think they're just being friendly.

Fake Protectiveness

Because their emotional insecurities are usually so obvious, fake protectiveness is less common with this personality. They just won't come off as being capable of protecting you. They want you to protect them! However, they may say extreme things intended to impress or charm you, and some of these may sound protective, such as "I would die for you." This is less likely to mean a lot if it comes from someone who seems over-reactive to so many situations.

So be attentive to warning signs of these four radar-jamming characteristics. The main things to watch for with this personality are the overstatements, overreactions, and over-the-top behaviors—all designed to lay claim to your attention. Just remember that these are not healthy or constructive behaviors. Someone who can be so extremely positive is just as likely to switch to being extremely negative at some point.

Blind Spots Where Histrionic HCPs Can Hide

So what are your own blind spots that would make you susceptible to this kind of personality? People who are very intellectual, academic, technical, or logical are sometimes attracted to the highly emotional aspects of histrionic personalities. (Engineers beware!) Dramatics seem to create a sense of balance, if you are someone who is not very emotional or emotionally expressive. In other words, the histrionic has all the emotions while you may have all of the rationality. But this is a mistake. In reality, you will be better off with someone with more balanced emotions.

Low Self-Esteem

If you have low self-esteem, you may find and tolerate a histrionic person, because they also seem to show a lot of self-doubts and distressed behavior. But they will eventually overwhelm you. As one survey respondent mentioned, in a statement that could apply to all of these dating situations:

Women with low self-esteem tend to "take what they can get."

Another person said she fell for her date's neediness, which often goes with the emotional insecurities of a histrionic person:

I think I thought I could maintain the boundaries. I realize now that my self-esteem was still so damaged from my failed marriage that I liked how needed this person made me feel. It was like a drug. Only I was the one addicted—he was the dealer.

Loneliness, Grief, Shyness

If you are lonely or grieving or shy, the emotional intensity of histrionic people can be very intoxicating, as the survey respondent said above. It can pull you out of your shell, but eventually you'll be overwhelmed by emotional chaos. If you're a back-of-the-room type who shies away from the spotlight, you may be more vulnerable to the seduction of the histrionic HCP. Since this can be a very subtle problem, remind yourself to look for it when spending time with a new, exciting person. Ask yourself: "Do our exciting emotions mean love, or is it the addiction of a histrionic HCP?"

I was lonely.

Offered security, and played on all my insecurities. Obviously pretended to be what he thought I was looking for, and when that persona started to fall apart and things didn't go his way or he wasn't the center of attention, all hell broke loose on me.

Naïve Beliefs

That brings us to another possible blind spot, which is the issue of mistaken beliefs, and particularly the idea that these warning signs are indications of true love. Emotional intensity can be very seductive, especially when mixed with sexuality. Step back from time to time to ask yourself whether you're falling in love or falling for drama. Also, ask your friends which they think it may be. If they have been around the person enough, they will probably notice if they seem over-the-top with their emotions, or frequently make extreme statements—things you might have a hard time seeing yourself, through the haze of romance.

There's another mistaken belief to watch out for—the idea

that you can change them and make them a better person. Histrionic HCPs often present themselves as so needy and suffering, they practically demand your assistance. It is easy to want to take care of them and save them from themselves. If you're a natural "helper" or "fixer," you will be tempted to do everything you can to intervene and make things easier for this person. It's natural to want to help, but ask yourself if you're working harder on their problems than they are. And furthermore, do they actually take your advice or accept your help? If not, you may be dealing with the histrionic HCP, and you might end up with a badly broken heart when they ride off with the next knight in shining armor. Remember these statements:

You cannot help someone by fixing them, and you cannot help someone who does not actually want to be helped.

Time and love will not change them.

You cannot change them.

If you start feeling the urge to jump in and rescue your partner, these statements should help you back up a few steps. It's very tempting to be a hero. But with personality disorders you have to have clear boundaries and hold people responsible for managing their own lives. It helps to realize that asking others to save them and make them a better person is common for all high-conflict personalities. And for dramatics, it's a defining characteristic. It's also important to remember that you can't actually save someone. This desire to help or save the partner is a common blind spot among people who fall into romances with histrionic personalities.

Here's an example of someone using clear boundaries with their histrionic partner:

I learned to have clear boundaries with my partner and she responded well. Boundaries given by me stopped her behaviors. I did it with kindness, firmness, no judgment, and 100 percent honesty.

People who grew up in alcoholic families or families with other addictions or mental health issues often have learned out-of-balance ways of handling relationship problems. As one survey respondent wrote:

Came to the realization that having grown up in an alcoholic family I had a codependent personality. I was going to fix her.

This is a very important insight. Getting into counseling or a recovery-type support group can help you develop this kind of awareness. Learning about your blind spots *before* you get into relationships with any of the high-conflict personalities may be very helpful in your life and save you many years of frustration.

Lastly, pay attention to relationship balance. You may have naïve beliefs that if you listen just a little bit longer, then you will get your share of attention. But that is not going to happen with histrionic HCPs. If it's out of balance, explore where the balance is off. It may be that your partner or prospective partner is driven by a fear of feeling ignored. If so, there will be no balance. Do they need to be the center of attention all the time? If so, it's time for some serious relationship reassessment.

Summing up these lessons learned from many people's years of painful experience, another survey respondent said this:

Relationships are about supporting one another, but you should never feel like you have to fix someone or that they are dependent on you to make things better. Also, if anyone mistreats you, regardless of their reasons behind it, they're not worth it.

In a relationship with a histrionic HCP, you will feel as if you are always listening, always helping, and always handing out the tissues to dry the tears—only to find that your efforts are wasted. Your partner continues down the endless path of drama, tears, and lies. You may be deeply committed to a person who seems as deeply committed to you, when in reality they have shallow, shifting emotions and a relentless focus on meeting their own needs.

Quiz: Are You Dating a Histrionic HCP?

Here's an informal quiz. It's not a scientific survey, but it can help you think about whether your partner might be a histrionic HCP. You can also take this test online: **www.dating-radar.com.**

Answer with a "1" for yes and "0" for no.

Your partner:

_____ Thrives on drama and being center of attention; shares dramatic, attention-getting stories.

_____ Leads with flirtation and sexuality, with you and with others; behaves provocatively.

_____ Bursts into tears, especially after having been caught in a lie.

_____ Lies to get your attention, and distorts reality with fiction.

_____ Sometimes acts helpless; pulls at your heartstrings to take care of them; talks about having been victimized or taken advantage of.

_____ Idealizes you, then becomes indifferent.

_____ Tells your secrets to everyone; promises you they'd never talk behind your back, then does exactly that; starts rumors.

_____ Jumps easily from one relationship to the next, claiming boredom.

_____ Doesn't notice when you try to change the subject or end the conversation.

_____ Shares too much personal information (about themselves or others).

_____ Wants to be taken care of.

_____ Complains about physical ailments; goes to the doctor (or other practitioners) more often than average.

_____ TOTAL

0	Green (mild)	Take the test again or ask a trusted friend for input, to be sure you're not missing something. If you get 0 again, go for it— but keep your eyes open.
1 - 3	Yellow (spicy)	Consider getting out now. If you're not ready to get out, proceed with caution.
4 - 12	Red (nuclear)	Don't commit to this person unless you're ready to sacrifice.

Conclusion

Life with a histrionic partner can be fun and exciting, but equally draining. You may find yourself pouring your time and energy into them without the favor ever being returned. Warning signs include lots of dramatic stories, intense but superficial emotions, and a willingness to expose your secrets and others' secrets in order to get attention. If you see your partner treating other people like this, assume that you will be treated the same way someday.

Histrionic HCPs can jam your radar with excitement and charm, as well as drawing you in to be a protector for them, to take care of their many problems. As with the other high-conflict personalities, sexuality can be an intense, driving force. It can lead you to share intimate information about yourself as part of relationship bonding. But when the intensity wears off your secrets may be revealed and you may be talked about dramatically in very negative terms.

It's essential to pay attention to your blind spots, so you do not get seduced by this excitement and sexual energy. Someone who is so intensely emotional and excited about you can be very pleasantly distracting from any feelings of low self-esteem, grieving, or shyness. If you develop a strong sense of your own identity and needs, you won't get swept away and then become a target of blame.

Lastly, resist the urge to try to change the person or, more likely, try to solve all of their many problems. If you are a natural helper or a technical type, you may be tempted to play this fixer role. Be forewarned and practice looking for balance, rather than intense emotional excitement.

CHAPTER EIGHT

Other High-Conflict Issues to Watch Out For

Now that you've read the previous chapters, you're equipped with dating radar that will help you identify some of the most problematic kinds of high-conflict relationship partners: narcissistic, borderline, antisocial (sociopath), and histrionic. And since you know how to spot the warning signs for these folks, you have the power to avoid them entirely or break off a relationship as soon as you realize what's going on. This kind of insight can save you years of misery. It can even save your life!

But those four types are not the only problematic partners in the dating pool. There are a few other potentially high-conflict issues and patterns to be aware of. Each of these can cause problems all on its own. They can also combine with each other or with the types of personalities we have already described, leading to additional dating misery. The four patterns we'll cover in this chapter are addiction, bipolar disorder, autism spectrum disorders, and paranoia.

Addictions

Addiction can make it nearly impossible to have a good relationship. Someone with an active addiction is just too compromised to be a good partner to you. Their world revolves around their need for the next "fix," making them self-absorbed, with little time or energy left for anyone or anything else—including you. And once they're under the influence, you will be hit by the shrapnel, whether they're addicted to substances (such as alcohol, illegal drugs, or prescription medications) or to behaviors (such as gambling, sex, or using pornography).

In a popular reality television show, *Intervention*, family members submit their alcoholic or drug-addicted loved ones to the show for an intervention. For most, the addict is nearly at the end of their life and the family at the end of their rope. The show convinces the subject that they are being filmed for a documentary on addiction, and they only discover the truth that it's an intervention upon arrival for their final documentary interview, when they find their spouse or partner, family, and friends awaiting them.

Along the way, viewers are exposed to the raw reality of addiction, its impact on others, and also the enabling behaviors of people in the addict's life. Inevitably, the romantic partner (when there is one) is hit hardest, and is finding it nearly impossible to maintain a lasting, balanced, healthy relationship. Their needs never take center stage as long as getting the next drink, injection, huff, puff, or hit is the addict's priority.

It's generally easier to spot an addiction problem than a personality problem, although neither comes with a color-coded label. Addiction is fairly obvious, especially if you, the partner, are not in denial about it.

With addictions, the pattern is progressive—it keeps getting worse, so long as the person is actively drinking, using drugs, or otherwise engaged in the addiction. People tend to continue with their addictions despite the punishing consequences. Addicts can lose their homes, jobs, and relationships. They may spend all of their own money and then begin stealing from their loved ones. It's hard for those of us who don't have an addiction to understand how someone could be so self-destructive, but there you have it.

Being the partner of an addict means sacrifice, plain and simple. Whether the addict is a closet drinker or a raging binger, partners suffer. They forgo any chance of a balanced, two-way relationship. They suffer embarrassment while they watch life savings disappear and property get destroyed. They stand by as the addict wrecks cars, frightens the children, and possibly dies or kills someone else.

Key Characteristics

What does it mean to have an addiction? Here are the defining characteristics:

1. Excessive use of the substance or behavior
2. Preoccupation with use of the substance or behavior
3. Inability to control one's use of the substance or behavior
4. Life consequences such as job loss, legal trouble, financial problems, health problems, or damaged relationships
5. Increased tolerance for the substance or behavior (needing more to get same effect)
6. Signs of withdrawal (physical and/or psychological) if the person stops using

Recovery from an addiction is usually a lifelong process that involves quitting the substance or behavior completely. Successful recovery often involves ongoing support groups, such as Alcoholics Anonymous and other 12-step programs. People with addictions usually say that they are "recovering," rather than "recovered," because it is a continual effort to live "clean and sober" and avoid a relapse. However, with recovery skills and committed personal growth, many people in recovery lead successful, normal lives in all other ways.

Spotting an Addict When You're Dating

Unless they are in recovery, people with an addiction generally try to hide their addictive behavior. But, by definition, they have lost control over this behavior, and it becomes increasingly difficult to hide it and its consequences.

When you're dating, your partner's addiction may be the hidden reason behind:

- Frequent, unexplained gaps in their schedules—for example, being late most of the time or canceling plans you've made together.
- Unexplained absences or disappearances lasting days or longer.
- Bizarre behavior, for which they make excuses. This can include things like losing their wallet, keys, or phone; getting lost; or having car breakdowns. Of course, scheduling issues, losses, and other mishaps can happen to anyone. The thing to watch for is an increasing pattern of these problems. That may be an indication that an addiction has taken over.
- An increasing insensitivity to your needs or existence. As one drug addict explained it: the drug became his lover, and his partner couldn't compete.
- Surprisingly hostile or out-of-character comments or behavior.
- Irritability, argumentativeness, or out-of-character aggressiveness.
- Sudden violence toward objects or toward you.

- Strange new friends coming and going.
- Secretiveness and lying. When caught, covering with new lies.
- Preoccupation with blaming others for their own problems—and denial about their own contributions to the situation.
- Making you feel guilty for asking about their problems.
- Unexplained bruises, cuts, or bumps.
- Leaving children unattended.
- Missing work, school, or events.

Essentially, we are describing yet another pattern of high-conflict behavior here. However, rather than being embedded in the person's personality, the problem is embedded in their addictive behavior. If they can stop using alcohol or drugs or engaging in other addictive behavior, then their high-conflict behavior may also diminish or stop, and the great person you used to know can make a reappearance.

Not always, though. Some addicts have a personality disorder that predated their addiction. Many people with high-conflict personalities are in a lot of pain but they don't know why. Typically, an unresolved trauma causes deep pain and anguish. The person then starts drinking, using drugs, gambling, or whatever as a way to numb the pain. Eventually, this problematic coping strategy becomes a full-blown addiction. For people who develop an addiction on top of a painful personality problem, just getting "clean and sober" may not have much effect on their high-conflict behavior patterns unless they simultaneously get help for their underlying personality problems and learn new relationship skills. But this requires them to acknowledge the personality problem in the first place—which, as you've learned, they are unlikely to do. It also requires a lot of time, commitment, discipline, and financial resources. And even with all of those things, many relationships don't survive.

Back to *Intervention*: In each episode a brief history of the addict's childhood and young adult years is shown. Approximately nine out of ten have some type of trauma in their background that's never been addressed or resolved. For many, it started with their parents' divorce, followed by some type of abuse—typically sexual abuse by a babysitter, relative, or someone else with a close relationship to the child. Their development is altered, with some developing high-conflict personalities, and their vulnerability to a future addiction becomes predictable and maybe inevitable.

Keep in mind that people with the personality disorders described in this book are more likely than the average person to have a substance abuse disorder. So you will meet some people with both a high-conflict personality and an addiction. On the other hand, there are many people with an addiction who do not have a personality disorder. Just be aware and use your radar when someone you're dating starts acting strangely—and then tries to explain the unusual behavior. Both addicts and people with high-conflict personalities often display similar behaviors: yelling, raging, violence, lying, and so on. If you knew them to have reasonable behavior before the addiction, then it's most likely that they don't have a high-conflict personality. If you've only known them as addicts, it may be harder to tell until they get clean or sober. That's why you have to be aware and protect yourself.

Whether their substance abuse problems are personality-based or rooted just in addiction, a relationship with an addict is going to be hard on you as a romantic partner. It's not easy to see the person you're in love with abusing their mind and body with substances. Broken promises, lonely nights, behavior changes, and everything else that comes with substance abuse are painful for you. And these things aren't exactly pleasant or healthy for your partner, either.

Remember, you can't rescue them by loving harder, ignoring the problem, or protecting and cushioning them. Those behaviors just keep them sick. Instead, read about addiction, intervention, recovery, and your role in it. Jeff Vondervan, an interventionist featured on *Intervention*, repeats this line to the family and friends involved in every intervention: *There is nothing we won't do to help you get better, but there is nothing more we will do to help this continue anymore.*

How an Addict Jams Your Radar

People who are actively engaged in addictive behaviors are often skilled at covering them up—at least for a while. You will see radar-jamming behavior similar to that of people with high-conflict personalities.

For example, charm is a frequent distraction. However, with an addiction, the charm may wear off much sooner than it does for some of the high-conflict personalities. That's because it is harder for someone to keep the charm going when they are under the influence. Early in the relationship, they may wine you and dine you—maybe with just a little too much emphasis on the wine. Someone who buys "drinks all around" may seem appealingly successful and generous. Their wild stories may be fun, until you realize that the person can't stop talking. In a sense, there is a narcissistic, self-absorbed pattern to the initial dating behavior of many addicts—and, at first glance, they can be kind of charming in the same way that narcissists can.

Fake or exaggerated compatibility sometimes shows up in addicts as well. We see them trying very hard to impress their partner right from the start. They'll go out of their way to show you how similar they are to you. Perhaps it's shared political views or enjoying the same sports activities. Since they know on some level that the downside of their behavior is going to show up sooner or later, they have to present an upside as fast as possible.

Overt sexuality can be common for those with an addictive pattern. Of course, sex and drugs can easily go together, because substances weaken a person's inhibitions. Sex often grows disappointing without the drug, and lousy sex—or the prospect of it—can be a trigger for relapse. But beyond that, sex seems tied to some of the same brain pathways as compulsive addictive patterns. Both involve chemical rewards in the form of dopamine. There can be an urgency to get the dopamine hit from sex, the same way an addict is driven by the dopamine reward from their addictive behaviors. You might also see an escalation of sexual behavior as the addiction progresses.

Fake protectiveness can show up in people with addictive patterns. Part of this behavior is the common bragging and desire to impress others with how wonderful they are at the beginning of the relationship. While your partner may say they will "have your back" and watch out for you, they also may want you to be the protective person for them. People with an addiction are known to be "dependent" on their substances or addictive behaviors. It's very easy for them to switch this dependency over onto a real live partner—sometimes in an almost parent-child manner. Guess who plays the child?

All of these characteristics can jam your radar. However, addictive behaviors may show up a lot earlier in the relationship than signs of a high-conflict personality on its own. If you understand these patterns, they may be less likely to catch you by surprise.

Here are some examples from our survey:

Very sexual; promiscuous. Abused marijuana and alcohol. Binged and spent all of their money and then blamed me when they had nothing left.

Alcoholism tendencies. Never ending his education. Always seeking the next "title" or "degree" to add to a resume he wasn't using for employment. Extreme porn addiction showed itself much later in the relationship—and it was always "my fault" for him being attracted to it. He either loved me or hated me, with no in-between—ever. Never once said "I'm sorry." I didn't realize until after the relationship was over that he'd never actually said those words.

As evidenced by these comments, addictive behaviors often go together with high-conflict behaviors, including blaming others and seeing things in black and white.

If the Person Is in Recovery

In recovery, an addict may be outgrowing some of the patterns we've described, and there may be less likelihood of their jamming your radar. Clearly, you don't want to be in a relationship with someone who is in the grip of an active addiction. But what if a dating partner tells you they used to be an alcoholic but don't drink now? Many recovering addicts can become very good relationships partners, because they have learned life lessons in a recovery program that the average person may never learn. It's all about how long the person has been recovering and how committed they are to kicking the addiction.

In the first year of recovery, they are advised by program counselors to avoid getting into new dating relationships, because the experience can be so destabilizing as to trigger a relapse. Or the relationship can be a distraction from their recovery, or the romantic partner may become the new addiction. After that, the more years of recovery they have, the more stable and reasonable they usually become. Again, someone who has many years of sobriety can be an excellent partner. So we don't mean to discourage you from dating people who are secure in their recovery. Just be cautious.

However, watch out for the person who says they are "recovered" and think they can handle occasionally drinking or gambling or doing whatever their "old" addiction behavior was. After working in drug treatment programs, Bill has seen many people go quickly downhill because of a relapse triggered by an exciting new romance. "I can control it now," an alcoholic may say to their new partner, as they order a drink for the first time in years. But if they are truly an alcoholic, they will need to avoid such use for the rest of their lives. This is true for reengaging with any addictive behaviors from the past. Be aware of this danger, and notice whether the person takes risks regarding their recovery.

You aren't doing yourself or them any favors by forging ahead with a relationship against the one-year guideline. It's there for a reason. But their addictive brain may be in charge, telling them that they're well enough to date you, and you might fall for it. Don't. Recovery is about discipline and taking direction. Help both of you by giving it time.

It's also possible that they have relapsed already and are now lying to you about it. Just abide by the one-year rule and keep your eyes open.

Blind Spots Where Addicts Can Hide

The blind spots that make us vulnerable to romance with an addict are similar to those that make us blind to other high-conflict personalities. Many of them have to do with being attracted to the idea that somebody needs us or wants us. In fact, alcoholism is where the term "codependency" got started. The addict and their partner get hooked into a dance of mutual dependence. The partner becomes dependent on the needs of— or control by—the alcoholic or addict. And some, fearing their partner will die, assume full responsibility for their partner's life. They become their life support system until they've sucked you dry.

Low self-esteem is a common characteristic of people who get hooked into relationships with chemically dependent people or those with other addictive behaviors. The desire to help someone like this can be very compelling. Addicts often seem like just ordinary people with a minor problem. (In fact, they are ordinary people with a very big problem.) "You know, you shouldn't drink so much," you might suggest at the beginning of a relationship. But soon you may find yourself covering up for the person (calling in sick for them at their jobs) and managing their life on a daily basis. It can feel like you're doing something really valuable for somebody. Except that we have learned that this is really "enabling" them to stay stuck in their addiction, because you're doing the work that they should be doing. Sure, it boosts your self-esteem, but it's a dead-end project. Unless the person is working on their recovery, your help reinforces their addictive behavior.

Likewise, if you're lonely or grieving or shy, you will need to be very careful not to engage with someone who shows warning signs of active addiction. A shy introvert who suffers anxiety in public situations might be attracted to a fun-loving, outgoing, gregarious person. That's fine unless substances are the source of the fun. Likewise, after suffering a loss or experiencing loneliness, the temptation to fall for an addict may be increased just to alleviate or distract from those negative feelings. Addicts are often looking for codependents to take care of them in life. It can be very tempting, but as with the personality disorders, the relationship usually doesn't work and may end badly.

Many addicts are great talkers and emotionally intense, so they can sweep you off your feet with their messages of devotion and dependency—on you and your relationship. Don't mistake the warning signs for love. Mutual dependency is different from two independent people who can join together to share mutual interests, care for each other, and love each other for who they are, imperfections and all. Dependency is more like an infant-parent relationship, which can never be fulfilled between two adults. (Sorry.)

It's tempting to get involved with an emotionally-engaging addict, and believe that you can help them get over their addiction. It's a scenario that involves our two most common culturally-naïve beliefs: that time will make them a better person and that you and your love for them will make them better. After all, you may think that you can see clearly what your partner needs to do. And that may be true, but you can't do it for them.

Fortunately, there are many good treatment programs now, as well as self-help support groups such as Alcoholics Anonymous, Celebrate Recovery, and other 12-step groups. Unfortunately, most addicts don't use these groups, because recovery is hard work. It's easier to just find a codependent who believes love will cure all.

If you think you may have a codependent pattern (you're drawn to taking care of others, including addicts), you can find help from groups like Al-Anon. Their messages fit well with overcoming blind spots—messages such as, *You're not the cause of the addict's behavior; you can't control it; and you're not the cure.* So, once again, here are the two lessons learned by our survey respondents and many others:

> *Time and love will not change them.*

> *You cannot change them.*

One man put it very simply:

> *I believed I could help her. I was wrong.*

About addiction in particular, we want to add that family history tries to repeat itself. So if you grew up in a family in which you had to take care of someone emotionally, such as an alcoholic father or mother, you will be particularly vulnerable to repeating your caregiving pattern if you get into a relationship with an addict or a high-conflict personality. It's really hard to see these dynamics from the inside, so check with your friends or a therapist to see if they think you are getting involved with someone who wants you to take care of them.

It's always a good idea to get some counseling before dating, especially if you have been in difficult relationships previously, or if you are grieving, lonely, or shy, so that you don't let these issues blind you. We want your dating radar to work well for you, but as we've repeated throughout this book, it's ultimately up to you.

Bipolar Disorder

Bipolar disorder, or manic-depression, involves another pattern of behavior that can contribute to a high-conflict relationship if the disorder is not understood and managed. There's an increased likelihood of bipolar disorder for some of those with personality disorders. For example, the large NIH study mentioned earlier in this book indicates that approximately 30 percent of people with borderline personality disorder also have bipolar disorder, and about 17 percent of those with narcissistic personality disorder also have bipolar disorder. Bipolar disorder occurs about equally in men and women. (Grant et al. 2008)

In our experience, people who don't have much background in understanding mental health issues are highly likely to pin a label of bipolar disorder on anyone who acts outside the normal range of human behavior. Countless times we've received requests for help for someone's "bipolar" family member, spouse, boyfriend, and so on. We believe this is because the term has been commonly used for the last twenty or so years and has become very familiar to the public. In the absence of real knowledge about other mental disorders, bipolar has become sort of a go-to label.

People with bipolar disorder behave in some of the same ways as people with personality disorders, and the impact on relationships can also be similar. The difference is that the chaos of personality disorders is relationship-based, whereas bipolar disorder is rooted in brain chemistry. People with personality disorders have a hard time relating with other people in a balanced way. People with bipolar disorders have the manic-depressive cycles described below *and* may also have a hard time relating with other people.

Key Characteristics

Here are some of the common characteristics of people with bipolar disorder, including some of the criteria listed in the *DSM-5*. We've emphasized the traits that may affect dating relationships. Part of the time, people with bipolar disorder are "up" (manic). And part of the time they're "down" (depressed).

Manic, for a week or more:

- High energy, outgoing and talkative. Exciting and dramatic.
- Meeting lots of people, going on buying sprees, taking sexual risks.
- Distractible; starts lots of tasks but may not finish them.
- Wants you to share in high-energy, risk-taking activities.
- Doesn't sleep much. You, as their partner with normal sleep needs, may become exhausted trying to keep up with them.
- May engage in conflicts with strangers, family members, friends, or you. Police may be called, because of loud or violent confrontations with others.
- Blames others (including you) for setting limits and spoiling their fun.
- Down in the dumps. Low energy, not much interest in anything. Depressed (for two weeks or more).
- Not sociable. Self-critical. Discouraged. May sleep a lot, or little. Hard time making decisions.

- Suicidal thoughts or actions. Higher risk of suicide than average person.

The overall dating relationship may be dominated by this endless cycle of the bipolar partner being a very exciting person, then a very immobilized person. Of course, there is a range of how severe these conditions may be. Many people get into relationships with bipolar people during the manic phase, because they are so exciting and energetic. They can be super-appealing for a while. (In fact, many entertainers are said to have had this disorder.) Then comes a depressed period, which may be mild or serious. But often, dating partners don't recognize the "down" part of the cycle as bipolar disorder. Instead, they think they did something wrong or that it was caused by stress at work or in the family.

Medications are generally helpful for bipolar disorder. But sometimes the person doesn't like their medications and stops taking them. Then, they may spiral out of control once again.

How Bipolar Partners Jam Your Radar

The main way your radar gets jammed by someone with bipolar disorder revolves around how exciting they can be. You may get swept up in the excitement, energy, and positive mood of the bipolar person. Charm, compatibility, and sexuality all have a strong pull in the whirlwind of activity that they can generate. In a manic phase, the bipolar person is less likely to be protective because of their risk-taking mindset. Instead, you may feel protective of your partner, because these high-risk activities make you feel concerned.

Blind Spots Where Bipolar People Can Hide

Potential blind spots with bipolar partners are the same as with the other high-conflict personalities: Your low self-esteem, grieving, loneliness, or shyness may pull you in to the positivity and excitement of the bipolar person in a manic episode. It's like a Hollywood movie, in which you get swept off your feet. Also, the culturally-naïve beliefs that time and love can change them, or that you can change them, may seduce you, especially in trying to pull them out of their depressed period. So here's your reminder:

Time and love will not change them.

You cannot change them.

On the other hand, if the person commits to getting mental health care, including a medication evaluation, there may be potential for the relationship.

Autism Spectrum Disorder

Autism and related disorders are a relatively new area of attention in high-conflict relationship behavior. Asperger's is now considered to be on this spectrum. The relationship difficulties are in social communication and social interactions. People with this disorder (primarily men, but some women, too) are often mistaken for being narcissistic, because they have a harder time recognizing what they are feeling, communicating, and connecting with their partners, which makes them seem self-absorbed and inflexible. But autism spectrum disorder is mostly about interpersonal wiring, meaning that people on the spectrum aren't as good at reading other people's signals—such as facial expressions, tone of voice, and moods.

Key Characteristics

Here are some common areas of relationship difficulty:

- Have a hard time understanding the dynamics of relationships and have unrealistic expectations.
- May have very high technical skills, but poor skills at interacting, making it difficult to meet partners in the first place.
- Their eye contact and body language may seem off. They may have a hard time reading other people's eye contact and body language.
- They may seem self-absorbed and narcissistic, but it's because they have difficulty connecting well with others, rather than because of a belief that they're superior.
- May have little interest in social activities.
- May be preoccupied with rules and easily upset by other people's rule violations.
- May express anger very loudly, not recognizing the impact it has on their partner.

As with all of the disorders mentioned in this book, there is a range of severity, and also a range of success in managing these problems. While people with autism spectrum disorder may generally function well at work and in less intense relationships, close relationships may be the hardest for them.

Here's how one survey respondent described her marriage:

Make sure you're educated about the signs for disorders such as high-functioning autism which cause a lot of bad behaviors and domestic violence situations; because after fifteen years of hoping it was just a mood disorder and would get better, my husband has been diagnosed with high-functioning autism, and so much damage has been caused that it's not reparable. Signs of anger and protectiveness and control, and misinterpreting situations and conversations, and withholding sex and money were some odd early signs I now recognize.

As with the intertwining of high-conflict personalities and substance abuse or addiction, people on the autism spectrum could also have a personality disorder or traits of one, especially if they experienced childhood trauma or a strong sense of entitlement as a child.

Paranoia

The *DSM-5* lists paranoid personality disorder as another disorder. We have not included it as one of the major types of HCPs, since some of this personality's extreme behavior shows up in all of the high-conflict personalities as excessive fearfulness. Whatever else might be going on, these paranoid behaviors can lead to high levels of conflict in their relationships.

For example, all of these high-conflict personalities anticipate betrayal, especially sexual betrayal. They may conclude that their partner is off having an affair whenever they are hard to reach.

People with paranoid personality may mistrust everyone else in your life and want you to separate from them and focus only on your partner. Because of the tendency to become isolated from the world with this type of personality, you may easily become cut off from your other friends and family members.

Key Characteristics

Here are some key characteristics of paranoid people that may cause difficulty:

- They are suspicious of everyone and trust no one completely.
- They anticipate being deceived or betrayed.
- They may wrongly think others are conspiring against them.
- They carry grudges and may plan to collect on them later.
- Because they fear being criticized or attacked, they may attack first (verbally, physically, with rumors, etc.).

How Paranoids Jam Your Radar

While it may seem that this personality would not be very alluring, they can make themselves attractive, and even charming, at first. They may appeal to their partners because of the appearance of compatibility of interests—in particular, a shared suspiciousness of others. In some relationships, the partners have a similar hostility toward other groups and share the same strong beliefs that their group is vulnerable in the world. The paranoid personality can be very appealing to people who feel they are ostracized by society. If everyone else is out to get you, the two of you can join together strongly in your shared paranoia about the rest of the world.

Overt sexuality does not stand out one way or the other with this personality. Protectiveness may be a large issue, as the person is preoccupied with protecting against and being protected from a hostile world. In some cases, they will ask you to commit to secrecy, and perhaps to spy on others in your own shared conspiracy. Someone who's paranoid may engage in a lot of controlling behavior in order to feel safe in the world and with their partner. Sometimes this behavior leads to domestic violence and other power and control dynamics.

Blind Spots Where Paranoids Can Hide

People with lots of paranoia can be very intense when they find someone who is interested in them; in fact, they may feel more strongly about the relationship than you do. If you have low self-esteem, you may be a very appealing romantic target for someone who wants to have a partner in becoming isolated from a scary world. Likewise, if you are grieving, lonely, or shy, you may be drawn in to their fervent desire to be with you. It's easy to misunderstand this kind of emotional intensity. As we have said throughout, it's wise to get counseling to strengthen your sense of confidence and thus become less vulnerable to this type of person. Remember, isolation combined with togetherness may cause you to mistake these warning signs for love.

You may slowly realize that the person is paranoid; that they see the world as a much more threatening place than most other people do. Watch out for the temptation to believe that you can soften their fears. This is one of those culturally-naïve beliefs. It's more likely that they will instead get you to heighten your own fears the longer you are around them. Remember:

Time and love will not change them.

You cannot change them.

Conclusion

These four additional high-conflict issues present major relationship risks. The basic patterns of addiction have a lot in common with high-conflict personalities: lots of blame, denial of responsibility, all-or-nothing thinking, and increasingly inconsistent behavior. Yet they can be charming, seem to have compatible interests, and may have an appealing sexuality. In addition, they can be very seductive of those who have low self-esteem, or who are grieving, lonely, or shy, and those who believe they can fix them on their own.

Likewise, people with bipolar disorder can be particularly exciting during their manic phase, with lots of outgoing social behavior and energy. However, the downside includes depression, increased risk for suicide, and blame toward others.

Those with autism spectrum disorders have a more biological problem, which includes a deficit of understanding normal interpersonal behavior. They don't seem to connect well, and as a result may seem particularly self-centered and insensitive to their partner's needs.

Paranoid personality disorder is one of the ten personality disorders that can become high-conflict personalities. Folks who are paranoid are suspicious of everyone, including their romantic partners. They tend to become isolated and want their partners to become isolated with them. These characteristics can show up in all four of the personality disorders we have been discussing.

In general, your dating radar should detect these issues, just as it will the other four personality types. Learn the patterns of behavior, beware of letting them jam your radar, and work on your blind spots—so that you are less vulnerable to becoming a romantic partner for one of these difficult personalities, or better informed if you do. Being out of balance is the common theme among all of the personalities and issues we've discussed in this book. Look for balance in your partners and in your relationships. Avoid extremes, especially extremes that show no sign of changing.

CHAPTER NINE

Splitting Up

Okay. So you've given it a few months or a year to see if Mr. Wonderful or Ms. Right is "the one" for you. Unfortunately, you have started to see lots of warning signs. It now looks like you're dating Mr. Trouble or Ms. Crazy. Good thing you developed dating radar! Your heart may be saying *yes*, but your gut says *no*, and you're wise enough to listen to your gut and apply your rational thinking.

Now what do you do? Typically, people in your situation want to get out. They want to split up before they get in any deeper, but they're afraid, they don't know how to get out, or they've tried and failed. Of course, if you want to continue on, that is your choice. Depending on the severity of the disorder, your skill at handling it (and taking care of yourself), and your partner's willingness to seek treatment (particularly those with borderline personality disorder), you may have chosen to stay in the relationship. If so, we wish every success to both of you. This chapter is about what to do if you decide you want to end the relationship.

You may think that you're moving on before the relationship becomes too serious. Keep in mind that high-conflict people take their relationships very seriously, even after just a few dates together. In their mind, the relationship is further along than it is in your mind. This is one reason why breaking up with an HCP is usually far more complicated than it would be with an ordinary person. Given their all-or-nothing thinking, unmanaged emotions, extreme behavior, and preoccupation with blaming others, a breakup may feel like a declaration of war to them. And when it feels that way to them, it probably will to you, too.

So, in this chapter, we'll talk about what you can do to keep yourself safe and minimize the fallout. We'll look at some of the possible extreme behaviors you may have to deal with. Then we'll cover special issues for each of the four high-conflict personality types. Remember, they are all preoccupied with intensely blaming others—which will now include you. Brace yourself!

Preparing Yourself for the Possible Reactions

Deciding to let go of a dating relationship with a high-conflict person can be agonizing, or it can be a relief. Now that you've decided to disentangle yourself, you need to be prepared for anything. Hope for the best, but prepare for the worst.

It's best to have a plan and to develop that plan with a knowledgeable advisor *before you tell your dating partner*. Ideally, this would be a therapist who understands high-conflict personalities and how they overreact to rejection. If you don't have a therapist available, you should at least consult with a few reliable people who know you and your dating partner, such as good friends or trusted family members. (It wouldn't hurt to ask them to read this book first, so they aren't as likely to be fooled by the HCP's charm, victim status, and stories).

High-conflict people generally have strong insecurities

about close relationships. This means that when you end the relationship, they are more likely than the average person to do something extreme—most likely something that is already part of their patterns of behavior. Keep in mind their fear-driven personality. You ending the relationship goes to the core of their fear. It will be important for you to have a plan for how to deal with your partner's reaction or resistance to the message that the relationship is over.

Let's look at some of the situations that might come up. And remember that, while our examples may highlight one gender or the other, none of the behaviors we discuss are gender specific.

Domestic Violence

The most extreme of these behaviors is domestic violence, which may include risk of injury or death. During a breakup is the time when people with high-conflict personalities can be most dangerous. If you watch the news, you'll see this reality all the time. The sad case of Nicole Brown Simpson is a good example. She was killed by her famous husband, O.J. Simpson, when they were splitting up. It seems that he may have become hopeful that they were getting back together again. Then he saw her with a male (nonromantic) friend and flew into a jealous rage.

The intense emotions for such a high-conflict person are most raw when they feel a threat to their sense of relationship security. As we will explain below, some of these personalities are more risky than others. But you should always be prepared for the threat of danger and sudden escalation into violent behavior when you're moving toward separating completely from a high-conflict partner. We'll talk about safety plans and restraining orders later in the chapter.

Destruction of Property

Some HCPs will react by destroying your property, including valued possessions. This can include slashing your car tires, smashing a car window, throwing your car shifter into a different gear while driving, destroying a favorite piece of clothing, breaking a favorite vase or lamp, and so forth. Some will cut up pictures of important people in your life, flush your (or their) wedding ring down the toilet, or destroy anything that they believe is meaningful to you. You have probably seen all of these and more in the movies.

The more dangerous HCPs, the nuclear ones, may do it to dominate you or feel superior to you. The mildly spicy version destroys property because they lack control of their impulses.

While an angry partner can wreck your stuff any time, when you're splitting up is when you're at highest risk—when they want to exert power and control over you to manage their own upset feelings.

Stalking

Both men and women have been known to stalk their exes. They may drive by your home to see if you're there and with anyone else. Some might even go through your trash to look for receipts or other evidence that you're cheating on them. They may show up at your workplace and make a scene. They may harass you online or try to hack into your social media account, email, or phone. At the very least, you should prepare by changing your passwords to something your partner couldn't easily guess.

Like the catfishers we discussed in chapter 3, HCPs may

also set up fake online profiles to stalk you.

But you must realize that stalking isn't necessarily a conscious effort by HCPs. (They don't think to themselves that stalking is on their to-do list.) Instead, think back to the core fears that drive them: fears of being inferior, abandoned, dominated, or ignored. Ending relationships with HCPs strikes the core of their core fear, which can prompt stalking behaviors.

Some even engage in stalking long before a breakup, if they suspect you're cheating on them or spending time with someone they don't like. Jealousy is a huge motivating factor. But as we saw with property destruction, when you're splitting up is when you're at highest risk of being stalked.

Harassing New Boyfriends or Girlfriends

High-conflict people lack normal boundaries, so if you get involved with someone else, the HCP ex may feel free to contact your new romantic partner and say awful things about you. In many instances, the HCP ex contacts the new love interest to describe in vivid detail some of the sexual experiences they had—sometimes with photos or video to go along with the stories. Technology has launched us into a new era in which HCPs have all sorts of tools to harass their ex or their ex's new love interests.

Your HCP ex may embarrass you at work or at family events. They may surprise you in public, when you're with a new partner. They may break into your car and leave embarrassing notes. In extreme cases, they may try to physically harm your new partner. For these and other reasons, it's good to try to finish splitting up with an HCP before becoming openly involved with someone else. Then, provide relevant information to the new person in advance so they're not blindsided at some point. You don't want to have to explain after the fact.

Damaging Your Reputation

How else can someone get relationship revenge in today's society? One of the worst is trying to ruin someone's reputation. Attempts are easily made on the Internet as well as in person. Out-and-out lies may be told. Confidences may be revealed— sexual secrets, family secrets. Or your ex may simply share distorted perceptions. They may tell your friends your "true" opinion of them, reveal your secret plans for future business endeavors, reveal your financial difficulties, and so on. It's common, almost an unwritten rule, for HCPs to send revenge porn to new partners, family, and friends—even the media. In fact, some people have taken their own lives over such revelations. The idea is to hit you where it hurts the most.

Fighting over the Kids

Hopefully, if you're going to split up, you'll split up before you have children together. However, realistically speaking, many people get pregnant and have children very quickly in relationships with high-conflict people. The "spark" that drew you together may lead to sex without protection, which often leads to one or more children. Or you may decide to have a child as part of the rush into a committed relationship.

Fighting over the children is one of the most painful aspects of splitting up with a high-conflict person. It's fairly common for HCPs to try to turn their children against the other parent and keep court battles dragging on for years, sometimes even after the kids have become adults. If you have kids together, it's especially important that you speak with a family lawyer and a therapist before you announce that you want to split up. There are many details that need to be planned for and handled in a very careful manner.

Financial Disruption

Sometimes a former romantic partner will try to ruin you financially. They may take your account numbers, or steal your credit card or ATM card. Some are charming enough to convince you to hand over access to your bank accounts, credit cards, or business records, or the key to your safety deposit box. Think of the news stories you've seen about people who have been secretly married to multiple partners at the same time and drained every one of their bank accounts. If you own a business or run a business, they may mess with your customers, suppliers, employees, and others involved. They can make a mess of your life beyond what you can imagine.

It's good to anticipate this possibility and build in protections, such as changing passwords regularly and never giving your partner access to your business and financial records—at least during the first year or so. If, within the first year of dating, your partner asks about your finances; requests access to bank, investment, or credit card accounts; or wants to merge bank accounts or handle your finances for you, it's a giant red flag to pay attention to. And it's always a good idea to remain active in all your financial matters at any stage of a relationship, so you will know when something doesn't smell right.

Personal Patterns

While all of the above scenarios are possible, the specific reaction really depends on the person. Your partner (or ex-partner) is most likely to act in ways they have in the past when very upset. Think back to what they did during prior crises in their lives, such as when the two of you had a major disagreement, or when they split up with previous partners, or had conflicts with close family or friends. And don't necessarily believe what they tell you about their history. Ideally, talk to people who have known the person for a long time and ask them to give you some tips.

A Field Guide to the Breakup Patterns of HCPs

While you should always be prepared to protect yourself from any of the reactions described above, including the worst of them, each personality has its own tendencies. It may help you in your planning to know what these are.

Narcissistic HCPs

Since narcissistic HCPs are all about being superior in the eyes of others, many of them will feel diminished and insulted when you break up with them. After all, you dared to embarrass them in the eyes of the world. In the narcissist's mind, there are only two kinds of people: winners and losers. Your act of rejecting them makes them look like a loser, when they are driven to look like winners. This can be humiliating for them.

A common response for narcissists is to humiliate you in return. This can happen even if you were careful not to actually humiliate them—because they are so afraid of being inferior, they'll feel humiliated anyway. They will find a way to prove that whatever led to the end of the relationship was *all your fault*. They will find a way to blame it on your inferiority, based on some deficiency in your personality or general behavior. They will say that you were stupid to break off the relationship with them. They may be very public about blaming you, as they are concerned that other people will get the idea that it's really their fault, and they can't tolerate that. So they have to quickly and effectively lift themselves up by putting you down. Narcissists may say things like, "She couldn't handle me," or, "He realized I was so much better than him."

But sometimes the opposite happens: they react as if the breakup (and maybe even your entire relationship) is completely insignificant. They take off and immerse themselves in another relationship. Sometimes this is someone they were already seeing during your relationship; you just didn't know it, although you may have suspected. Narcissists like to have lots of attention and admiration, so they're always on the lookout for new sources of attention and admiration, such as new partners. Some of them have two or three relationships going at the same time. This adds up to a scenario in which they can act as if you splitting up with them doesn't matter at all.

Sometimes, the narcissist will save you the trouble of initiating the breakup by deciding that they want to split up with you. Usually this is because they are already moving on to someone else—someone with more status. (Remember that narcissists are drawn to anyone who they think reflects well on them.) In this case, it may be your lucky day! Don't resist it, if you think they have a high-conflict personality. It's always easier if it's your partner's idea. You just have to cope with your own vulnerabilities to rejection. Better to talk this through with friends or a therapist, rather than to try to talk an HCP out of rejecting you. It may not feel like it at the time, but being dumped by a narcissist could be the best thing that ever happened to you.

Overall, it's generally easier to split up with a narcissist than with one of the other high-conflict personalities. As soon as the two of you break up, you'll end up in the "loser" category, and narcissists don't want to waste their energy on people they see as losers.

Borderline HCPs

People with borderline personalities have a strong fear of abandonment, which causes an equally strong need to remain connected to you. It's almost as though you are the oxygen supply for the two of you. Therefore, they will be extremely upset when you split up with them. In fact, they will feel as if they can't breathe. They usually resist the breakup with intense sadness, fear, or anger—and behavior to match. Some will try to cling desperately, until it's clear that it won't work. (This may be where you'll experience stalking behaviors.) Then, they will go into a rage and may assault you physically, verbally, or financially. The intensity of both their clinging behavior or their raging behavior can be shocking. Many on the other side of borderline HCP rage use the word diabolical, or say things like, "I've looked the devil in the eye and survived to tell about it." And many borderline HCPs say they actually see red when they rage.

People with borderline personalities often go public with their anger and may spread rumors, publicly confront you, or try to draw in your family, friends, and others to take their side against you. In some cases, the people in your life may get bombarded with mysterious texts, calls, emails, or letters in support of the HCP and against you, only to later discover they were all coming from the HCP themselves. They will do everything they can to get revenge and vindication.

As with each of the HCP types, these are mostly unconscious, fear-driven actions. If you think they're out of their mind to do some of these things, well, they are—at least, they're out of their logical minds for the time being. Unfortunately, their attachments are very powerful, even if you've only dated them for a few weeks. So be prepared for a storm of anger and revenge.

You may feel tempted to soften the blow by having a long talk with them about still being friends, or about how much you did care about them when the relationship was going strong. However, this just intensifies their emotional connection with you and makes it harder for them to let go. It's better to move consistently out of their lives, although you may do it slowly so as not to make it too powerful of a jolt. Just don't reverse yourself in the middle of emotionally withdrawing, or you may reinforce their desperate efforts to try to win you back.

This can be the hardest or one of the hardest personalities to split up with. That's why it's so important to wait a year before making a major commitment to them. They often want to get married quickly, to sooth their fear of abandonment, so that, itself, should be a warning sign. Try to resist for a year, during which you will usually see other signs of high-conflict behavior.

Sometimes it helps to meet with your partner at a therapist's office to tell them you want to split up. The assistance of the counselor may help them process the information. However, the biggest help is usually time—although it can take a long period of time for them to emotionally move on—or a new relationship. Often, they may meet someone new and drop you like a pancake, attaching to their new love interest just as quickly as they once attached to you. You'll want to pray they meet someone new, but you'll also have to pray *for* that someone new.

Antisocial HCPs

Antisocial, or sociopathic, HCPs are generally less invested in their relationships than the other HCPs and often move on before you are even ready to let go. However, if you are the one to do the leaving, keep in mind that they can also be quite dangerous. Conning or violence may be part of their repertoire. Your own hopes and expectations about the relationship may blind you to the reality that they truly don't care about you. It's a hard pill to swallow, especially if you've invested time and emotion in them.

You will probably already know about their breakup patterns, before you break up with them yourself. Why? Because they've likely bragged to you about how they put their exes in their place. Listen up when dating partners talk about past relationships and how they handled their breakups. Their explanations can be bristling with red flags.

Sociopaths really do not like to be dominated or controlled. So talking about respecting their freedom and their drive to be successful in their lives may be very helpful when splitting up with them. Always think back to their core fear of being dominated and plan your actions and how you manage the end of the relationship to work off of that fear. Even if you're worn out after a destructive relationship with them, try to summon the energy to manage your way out of the relationship.

But that's easier said than done, because this personality can be the meanest and most deceptive. On the surface they may act unfazed by you breaking up with them. However, underneath or in hidden ways, they may be plotting how to get back at you for this, perhaps days or weeks later. In our consultations with partners of antisocial HCPs, the common thread is a deep-seated fear that their ex will exact some awful revenge.

The nuclear sociopath can be quite dangerous, so you should listen to your gut and pay attention to your rational thoughts. Read the chapter on antisocial HCPs again. If you recognize your partner in it, take action to protect yourself. Inform your family, friends, work colleagues, and neighbors of the potential behaviors that could occur and ask them to help keep watch over you. If you are concerned for your safety, talk to domestic violence advocates or law enforcement officials for advice. Your safety—as well as the safety of your kids, if you have them—is the priority.

Histrionic HCPs

Histrionic HCPs are very dramatic, so they usually feel compelled to draw attention to themselves whenever things don't go well—and a breakup would certainly be one of those times. Remember, their core fear is of being ignored. They are likely to be very public about how terribly you treated them. You may be amazed at how far their opinions and emotions will reach. Many people will probably believe them, because they pack such strong emotions into their complaints about you.

Generally, histrionic HCPs won't become violent, but you should always remain aware just in case there is some overlap with the other HCP types. For example, they may be a little histrionic and a little borderline. So even if you think a histrionic HCP won't get violent, always be aware and prepared just in case they have other things going on that you didn't previously spot. The true histrionic HCP will usually move on quickly to become the center of someone else's attention and it won't take them long to find the next vulnerable person who needs someone to take care of.

Again, for all four of the HCP types, you can tie their behaviors back to their core fear to understand the path to the end.

Narcissistic HCP	
Core fear:	Being inferior
When you break up with them, they feel:	Inferior
So they have to:	Feel superior again
And they may do it by:	Blaming you Raging at you Humiliating you Lying Being violent Destroying property Acting like you never existed/dismissing you Threatening lawsuits Blasting sex videos or nude pictures of you through social media or other means

Borderline HCP	
Core fear:	Being abandoned
When you break up with them, they feel:	Abandoned
So they have to:	Feel attached again
And they may do it by:	Blaming you Stalking you Raging at you Being violent Destroying property Threatening suicide Rage driving Telling distorted versions of the truth Threatening lawsuits Getting revenge Turning people against you Blasting sex videos or nude pictures of you through social media or other means

Antisocial HCP	
Core fear:	Being dominated
When you break up with them, they feel:	Dominated
So they have to:	Feel dominating again
And they may do it by:	Blaming you Being violent Lying about you Dismissing you Humiliating you Pretending they never knew you Blasting sex videos or nude pictures of you through social media or other means

Histrionic HCP	
Core fear:	Being ignored
When you break up with them, they feel:	Ignored
So they have to:	Feel like the center of attention again
And they may do it by:	Blaming you Telling distorted versions of the truth Exposing your "secrets"

Again, we caution you that many HCPs don't have just one HCP type; they may have a combination of two or more, and they could have other issues (such as substance abuse or paranoia) as well. So no matter what type you think your partner is, always be prepared.

The High-Conflict Person's Grieving Process

Once you've ended things, you may feel just plain relieved. The relationship that has caused you so much misery is finally over! However, it may not *really* be over until much later. That's because it's not just about delivering the bad news and then going through your own normal steps of letting go. That's difficult in ordinary relationships. It's exceedingly difficult in HCP relationships. The high-conflict person also has to go through their own very difficult way of managing loss. They don't go through the grieving process in the typical way. The breakup is not all the way over until they stop trying to get you back or to get revenge for you splitting up with them.

The normal grieving process has five stages, according to Elisabeth Kubler-Ross, who wrote about death and dying fifty years ago (Kubler-Ross 1969). Since then, we have learned that the loss of a relationship can be just as devastating. The stages are:

1. Denial (It can't be happening to me.)
2. Anger (If it is, I'm mad as heck and will fight this every inch of the way.)
3. Bargaining (Trying to negotiate out of the inevitable loss.)
4. Depression (Turning inward and feeling the pain.)
5. Acceptance (You remember, but the memories don't stop you in your tracks anymore.)

HCPs typically get stuck in the anger stage. They keep fighting against reality and telling their stories to anyone who will listen. But they don't really get relief by telling their stories, so they are stuck in the past, repeating and repeating to others how awful you have been toward them. It's a wound that never heals. They remain stuck in a self-defeating loop that not only holds them back but can also harm you.

Keep this in mind when you think they should be over it

(you) by now. Breakups can be much harder for HCPs than for the rest of us, and you can't talk them into "getting over it."

A Step-By-Step Guide to Splitting Up

Needless to say, splitting up with a high-conflict person won't be as easy as a text message. (We definitely don't recommend that approach with HCPs.) Ideally, you will say or write things to them that are respectful and relatively unlikely to trigger extreme emotions—although many high-conflict people are prone to strong emotions by definition, so they may get very upset regardless of what you do. Let's break it down step-by-step.

Anticipate the Reaction

Start by anticipating how your dating partner will react to the news. Think back on situations when they were confronted with unwelcome news or some sort of rejection. How did they respond? Have they told you how their previous relationships ended? This gives you an idea of how they might react to a breakup.

You may be dreading their reaction, but logically anticipating it will give you more confidence because you'll feel more prepared and thus more in control. Develop your strategy and plan for it as seriously as you would plan a project at work. Remind yourself of your goal to end the relationship and figure out the right approach to do so.

Rehearse Your Lines

How will you break the news? It's important to think carefully about the best way to say it's over.

You might say, "I've been doing some thinking about my relationship with you and realized that we probably aren't the best fit. There's no easy way to do this, but we need to move on and go our separate ways. I'd really like for you to find a relationship that *will be* the right fit for you, and I wish you well in your future." However, this is only a suggestion. Don't use these words if they don't feel natural to you, or if you feel unsafe saying them.

Avoid criticizing your partner. Your abandonment itself may be overwhelming enough for them. Don't tell them they're a jerk or an a—hole, or that you hope they'll rot in hell, as tempting as that maybe (and as good as it might feel to say it). Remember, getting out of an HCP relationship can be a risky time, and it is a process that must be *managed* by you. If you are vengeful, it will backfire on you. Instead, don't act on emotion. Act on logic.

Avoid criticizing yourself, too. You don't want to feed their all-or-nothing thinking, such that they believe it's all your fault and then tell this to everyone you know.

It can help to practice your lines with your therapist, if you have one, or with a friend you trust, but only if you've educated them about your partner's high-conflict personality. They may be fooled by the HCP's charm, or they may have never been around someone like this, so they might give you bad advice unless they have at least some basic information about HCPs.

Choose Your Setting

Next, think about where to deliver the news. It's important to think about the possibility of an extreme reaction. In most cases, it shouldn't be that dangerous, especially if you have only been dating for a short time, so it may not matter much exactly where you do it. But if you think the situation might be volatile, do it with someone else with you, such as a counselor, friend, or family member. That way you'll have some protection and a witness if your partner makes false allegations against you later on. And if you think they might react with violence or other extreme behavior, have someone else give them the news for you while you're in a safe place, such as a faraway friend's home, women's shelter, or other location.

Let Them Down Easy

Except in dangerous situations, it can help to back off in steps, so that they don't feel an extreme jolt all at once. It may be best to ease yourself out of the relationship. You can say that you are busy when you would have gotten together, then let them know it's really not going to work out as a relationship. If you're living together or have other entanglements, the process will be more difficult, and it would be best to consult with an attorney.

Be Ready for "Hoovering"

Your partner may try to win you back. The term "hoovering" has been applied when someone with a personality problem tries to manipulate you by "sucking you back in" to the relationship, like a Hoover vacuum cleaner. This can be done by trying to seduce you, by threatening to kill themselves, by saying they're pregnant, or through some other manipulation. Be prepared for this, and matter-of-factly say no.

Let Them Save Face

You will want to end the relationship in a way that helps your partner save face. If you're angry, don't try to destroy them just for a sense of satisfaction. But if you are sad or exhausted, don't try to talk them into feeling sorry for you at this time. Just be matter-of-fact and respectful in the splitting up process. Focus on what they need to know in a way that is as nonthreatening as possible.

Don't tell the world that you were dating an HCP. Just keep that kind of talk to a few really good friends. If word gets out that you are bad-mouthing your former partner, they may come back into your life with a vengeance. Let them go in peace.

Stick to Your Decision

Breakups with HCPs can go on forever if you allow them to guilt you into feeling sorry for them. Some will suddenly and magically have a serious "medical condition," while others will convince you they'll be homeless without you or that they'll kill themselves. Others produce an engagement ring or say they were going to propose "next week." These are all fear-based actions meant to keep you in the relationship. Ultimately, it's not good for either of you to fall for these behaviors and remain in the relationship to prevent their pain, condition, or whatever. When you give them clear boundaries, you're giving them a gift—and you're giving yourself one as well.

Breaking up really can be hard to do. When we're in a relationship, we're under the influence of all kinds of feel-good hormones like oxytocin and dopamine, especially in the first six to twelve months. We can get attached to someone, even if that person isn't good for us. And the prospect of being single again can be scary or unpleasant. After all, most people would rather not be alone. But, as you've learned, a relationship with a high-conflict person is going to be unhappy at best and perhaps even dangerous. So once you've made the decision to go, just go, and don't look back. If you think you might be at risk of reconciling with the HCP out of sadness or loneliness over the breakup, make a plan with a good friend who can give you some extra support for a while. We wish you the best!

A Word About Restraining Orders

In some cases, the person really, really won't let go and may show up at your workplace, at your home, or at your parents' home—possibly letting you know they are stalking you by dropping creepy little hints. And there's always the possibility of a violent reaction. So, when you're breaking up with a high-conflict person, should you get a restraining order (also referred to as an order of protection in some jurisdictions)?

A problem with a restraining order is that it usually means you will be in court together for a hearing about the order, and being in the same place at the same time is probably not the direction you want to be going in. It's a judgment call, whether engaging with a restraining order is good idea, or whether disengaging without one may be better.

If your partner has ever been violent toward you, getting a restraining order may be the smart thing to do. However, a restraining order does not stop a knife or a bullet, so you also should develop a safety plan: a place to go that's safe, some money tucked away as needed, and contact numbers if you have to suddenly leave the area or get help to come to you.

In cases of domestic violence, or if you're at all unsure whether a restraining order is right for you, we encourage you to talk this over with a lawyer, counselor, law enforcement agent, or court clinic that specializes in domestic violence restraining orders.

Conclusion

We don't want to scare you, but we want to warn you about all the ways high-conflict people may react to being rejected. Again, we think it's wise to hope for the best and prepare for the worst. One of the key factors is how deep you have gotten into the relationship. This is one reason we recommend waiting at least a year before making any big commitments. If you never had kids, got married, or even lived together, then there are probably few issues that will need your ongoing attention. You just need to be sensitive to the fact that splitting up with an HCP will be a process, rather than an easy "Bye." But if you give clear messages and keep a cool head, you'll have a good chance of being successful over time.

If you have made deep commitments, such as getting married and having children, and are now splitting up, then you should read Bill's book, coauthored with Randi Kreger, titled *Splitting: Protecting Yourself While Divorcing Someone with Borderline or Narcissistic Personality Disorder.* It covers a lot of the issues, including hiring professionals, preparing for court, and dealing with an angry ex in the process. If you decide to stay with someone who has borderline personality disorder, you may want to read Megan's book *Bait & Switch: Saving Your Relationship When Incredible Romance Turns Into Exhausting Chaos.*

Relationships with high-conflict people rarely improve over time. It's much more common for them to get worse. So whether you decide to leave or stay, be sure to get lots of support and consultation along the way.

CHAPTER TEN

Fine-Tuning Your Dating Radar

One thing we often hear from people who've been in high-conflict relationships is: "I wish I'd known all of this a year ago—or ten years ago!"

The problem for us (and frustration, frankly) as experts in the field is how to get people to pay attention *before* the relationship begins, instead of after the disaster. So, if you're youngish and new to the world of dating—pay attention. If you're divorced or have been in a disastrous relationship in the past—pay attention.

Most people develop dating radar through experience, if they develop it at all. You can think of this as the "school of hard knocks." To graduate from this institution, you have to make a lot of mistakes; that's the only way to learn to make fewer mistakes in the future. But by the time they have their degree in dating radar from the school of hard knocks, some people are mired in miserable marriages. They're deep in relationships that are difficult (although not truly impossible) to get out of. They're forever obliged to co-parent with somebody who makes everything infinitely more difficult than it needs to be.

A public example of this scenario is the high-conflict divorce and custody battle of reality-TV star and founder of the lucrative Skinnygirl brand, Bethenny Frankel. Viewers of the reality show she's on, *Real Housewives of New York*, have witnessed her dating life, married life, and divorcing life. Several years into the long, drawn-out, expensive war (divorce) she lets her guard down to her group of friends and spills her guts about her new (non-TV) reality—her living hell. She says:

I'm in a dungeon. I went with my heart and my gut and I never could have imagined what would happen. I'm in a very, very negative, torturous situation and I'm holding on by a thread. I'll never be done [with it].

Hopefully you'll never know [what this is like].

It's not in your gut or your heart…you have to be f——ing smart, because I'm in goddamned hell. Hell! And it won't end. It'll never end. I don't know why I'm being punished this way. My custody situation is over. My financial settlement is over. My apartment is sold, and yet I sometimes feel hopeless and I sometimes feel like my ex is untouchable and I'm not going to get out of this. If someone's life is to torture you, you're not going to be okay. I wish someone would have pulled me out.

The confession came about as part of a conversation with one of the other women in the group who was to be married in two weeks to a man who'd been repeatedly caught cheating on her. Bethenny's begging her to pay attention, be smart, listen to her friends! Get out before it's too late! Listen! But her friend ignores the warning, stating that she and her fiancé are happy and she's not looking in the rear view mirror; instead, she's looking straight ahead through the big wide windshield. No dating radar for her!

We want to help you develop dating radar ahead of time, without having to suffer. You can avoid a lot of mistakes by learning from the experience of so many others—experience that we have shared throughout this book. Before you buy a car, invest in the stock market, buy a house, you do a little exploration and background checking before making the purchase or investment. Before you commit to a partner, shouldn't you do at least as much research as you do when you're buying a cell phone?

There's a company called LifeLock that helps protect consumers from identity theft. They make this statement and promise on their website, www.lifelock.com:

> *There are many ways for criminals to steal your identity. They can open accounts, buy properties, and even file tax returns in your name. There's a new victim every two seconds, so don't wait to get protection.*

We could just as easily apply the same concept to your love life:

> *There are many ways for people to destroy your heart. They can dominate and control you, rage at you, demean you, abuse you, stalk you, and even steal your money and turn your family against you. There's a new victim every two seconds, so don't wait to get protection.*

Just as a service like LifeLock works to protect you from identity theft, Dating Radar works to protect you from relationship disaster.

We're no longer in the dark ages. Relationships don't have to be a mystery any more. But it's up to you to develop your dating radar—and then use it. Now that you have read all of the information we've laid out in this book, we want to help you get used to applying it. Let's put it all together now.

Blind Spots

We'll start with blind spots, because this is something you can work on right away. You can discover your vulnerabilities even when you're not in a relationship. In fact, that may be the best time to do it!

As you saw throughout this book, our survey respondents revealed that their top blind spots were:

- Low self-esteem
- Loneliness, grief, or shyness
- Mistaking warning signs for love
- Believing time and love would change the person
- Believing *they* could change the person

We'd like to say a little more about how you can learn to see better into these blind spots.

Low Self-Esteem, Loneliness, Grief, and Shyness

Many people get into a relationship with a high-conflict partner because of a combination of self-esteem problems, shyness, loneliness, or grief. It can be tempting to look to a romantic partner to solve these problems for you, but they can be better handled with a counselor than with someone you're dating.

If you are fairly new to the dating world, because you are young or have recently gotten out of a long relationship, it's worthwhile to examine your beliefs about yourself and about relationships. Do you feel that it's essential to always be paired up with someone? Do you feel, deep down, that you don't really deserve to be treated well? Seeing a counselor, at least for a few sessions, can help you get to the bottom of these things. It may save you a lot of angst in the long run.

Learning to separate your issues from other people's issues

will go a long way toward shrinking your blind spots. For instance, suppose you had a former partner who was very critical of you. The excessive criticism may reveal more about the former partner than about you. Maybe it's that she was just a very critical person, and not that you were deserving of so much criticism.

Or let's say that a former partner told you that you have an anger problem—that you couldn't cope with anger in that relationship. You might really doubt yourself now, and your self-esteem may have taken a hit. If it's possibly true, you should get some counseling, clarify the problem, and, if necessary, learn how to better handle anger.

But it may be that your former partner was the one who really had the anger problem—going into rages that no one should have to cope with. So, separating that out—what's my problem and what's someone else's problem—will be important. If you know what's about you and what's not, you'll be more confident holding the line with a future partner who acts up or tries to manipulate you.

Another approach to dealing with the low-self-esteem blind spot is to develop phrases or statements that you can repeat to give yourself encouragement. When you feel more secure about your own value as a person, you won't be as vulnerable to a high-conflict person. Here are a few to try:

I deserve respect and affection in my relationships.

Criticism from my partner says more about them than it does about me.

Life is short. I don't have to accept unacceptable behavior.

There's a good relationship for me out there. I'm going to find it!

And the best one of all:

Would I want my best friend to marry this person that I'm considering spending the rest of my life with? If the answer is no, then the answer is also no for me.

Sometimes we make the same mistakes over and over. Keep in mind what one survey respondent said:

Honestly, it took me a while to break a pattern of relationships with men just like this. I was aware of the pattern before I entered the relationship, but I hoped that the relationship was different and I had met someone different. I soon realized that I was repeating the same pattern, though. I was learning slowly. Over a course of five to ten years I did a lot of work on myself. I eventually broke the pattern and met a stable, loving man who I am in a committed relationship with now.

Remember that you don't have to go to the school of hard knocks! The key here is in recognizing your own patterns. That will help you change who you pick to be with, if that's an issue for you. It will also change how you deal with difficult times—for instance, when you are lonely or grieving and thus maybe inclined to settle for less than you deserve. Self-knowledge will also help you feel more confident in meeting and dating men or women who are ready for a good, solid relationship. And, if you've honed your dating radar, you'll be able to get out of a relationship quickly if necessary.

Don't look for a partner who will lift your low self-esteem. You need to learn how to do that yourself. When your self-esteem is solid, you will look for a partner who is reasonable, not someone who shows that they're out of balance by promising to make you whole. You need to be whole before you start looking. The same could be said for shyness, loneliness, or grief.

Your relationship will be healthier if you're not expecting your partner to solve these problems for you. Unfortunately, we have seen many people who seek their "better half." If you're hoping for someone to complete you, you're actually setting yourself up to attract a high-conflict person who will con you into believing they will "fix" you and "protect" you. It's harder for someone to con you if you see yourself as okay already.

Mistaking Warning Signs for Love

Our culture misleads us in many ways. The songs, the movies, the TV shows—they portray bad relationship behavior as if it's actually a sign that the person really, really cares. With enough exposure, you can start believing it. Getting over this takes re-educating yourself.

Here are some of the warning signs of high-conflict behavior that people may mistake for evidence of love:

Stalking: Following you around or driving by your house repeatedly is *not* a good thing. It's a warning sign of obsessive behavior, often associated with high-conflict people who have a special fear of abandonment or a need to dominate someone (you). You want a partner who can be upfront about their interest in you without sneaking around.

Constant contact: Sending you dozens of texts each day or calling you repeatedly at work is *not* a positive behavior in the long run. Sure, some of this is common during the first few days of an exciting new relationship. But it's not healthy weeks or months into the relationship. It's a sign of an unhealthy dependency on you, which can easily turn into a power and control dynamic, in which the person tries to cut you off from everyone else, including friends and family members.

Domestic violence: Unwelcome physical or sexual contact is *not* healthy. It is a serious warning sign. Consenting adults can do a lot of things, but it has to be by consent. If you let a pattern of hitting, punching, biting, shoving, forced sex, and so forth, get started, there will surely be more violence to come. It usually starts out ambiguously ("Did you mean to hit me, just then?" "Oh, it was just a love pat." Really!) If it was unwelcome, insist that it stop. And if it doesn't, get out as soon as you can.

By the way, this unwelcome behavior can be by men or women. If it's unwelcome, it's not okay, regardless of who's doing it and regardless of who's bigger or smaller. No one should have to put up with that from their partner.

Now, you may wonder about "friendly" assaultive behavior, as in some books and movies, where someone ravishes a swooning partner or shows the intensity of their desire by allowing themselves to be degraded. The key words are "unwelcome" or "consent." Early in a relationship with someone you don't know very well, pushing these limits can amount to playing with fire. It's best to leave playful dominance and submission out of the dating phase of the relationship. Save it for a few years later, when boundaries are clear and power is solidly equal in the relationship. *Then* you can let yourself be "taken," once you trust that your partner fundamentally has your best interest at heart and will respect the limits of your consent.

Mutual dependence: HCPs generally have dependent personalities, in that they want to make the relationship secure by having power and control over their partners, rather than by being equals. At first, it may seem harmless when they want you to take care of them excessively, or want to take care of you excessively. In the long run, though, they want you to bend to their lives without reciprocating. So, again, this is a warning sign, not an indication of true devotion.

A healthy relationship is an interdependent partnership of equals, people who can divide up tasks and do things for each other (you cook, I'll repair things; or you shop for this, I'll shop for that). The key is that the partners are independent people *choosing* to be together rather than *desperate* to be together.

Many of us grow up in religious institutions that put men in a position of dominance over women, suggesting that women must submit to men. Unfortunately, HCPs can grasp this teaching and use it to justify their dominance and feelings of superiority. Some even believe it gives them the right to abuse women. However, more religious institutions are changing their stance on the subject of late, after studying the scriptures systematically and in their original language. They are teaching now that marriage is a 50/50 arrangement and one gender is not more important than the other; each partner has duties and responsibilities. Some faiths teach that because someone has to make a final decision when there's disagreement, the man is given authority to do it; however, that decision-making authority comes *only* with protection of the woman's heart and being.

That spark: To build a strong relationship, you do not want to go around hunting for that "spark." The majority of our survey respondents felt a spark with their high-conflict dating partners right away! This is a way that they jam your radar, something we will discuss below. But *looking* for a spark is a blind spot that *you* should watch out for. You may be looking in the wrong places if you think you have to start out with a spark, or chemistry, or great excitement.

In cultures with arranged marriages, most partnerships work out well, even though the couple barely knew each other when they got married. Their love grows during their marriage, rather than on the basis of a spark at the start. Ironically, in our culture people have the most intense feelings at the beginning, and when those feelings fade, they may conclude that something's wrong and fail to appreciate the deeper love that can grow over time. So watch out for "the spark"—it can blind you so badly that you start down the wrong path.

Other warning signs: There are an infinite number of warning signs that can be mistaken for love. Don't be convinced that unwelcome behavior is acceptable. HCPs can be very persuasive and cause you to doubt yourself. It's their pattern of behavior over time that matters; that's what helps you sort out the high-conflict partners from the reasonable ones.

Make sure that you have people you can check in with, to help you get clear on what behavior is okay with you and what is not. Sometimes getting a second opinion can make the difference between life and death.

Of course, in talking about these warning signs, we don't mean to scare you. We have seen terrible situations, but we also know many people in very good relationships. We want you to be aware of the full range of what's possible. The more aware you are, the better you will be at staying safe and finding the love you want. All of these warning signs can be discussed in counseling or with your friends or family. We weren't trained for this growing up, and the larger culture gives us many mixed messages. Be aware of your vulnerabilities, and do not give in to unwelcome behavior disguised as love.

Believing That Time or Love (or You)
Will Change the Person

As if it's not bad enough that we've been taught to mistake warning signs for true devotion, there is another way that our culture has done us a disservice: by giving us the idea that "time and love" cures all. Also, we have been told, directly and indirectly, that we should be able to change our partners for the better. Well, we are two professionals who can tell you that this "just ain't so!" Forget about it! People don't change very much, except in the movies, in songs, and on TV.

It's widely accepted that no one person can cure an alcoholic or addict. They need a program of recovery, and they need to become motivated to work on their recovery—every day. Essentially, addicts have to treat themselves with ongoing recovery. It's the same thing with people with high-conflict personalities. Unless they are working on themselves in an intensive program, they will not change. And few of them have any interest in changing, because they don't see that they have a problem in the first place. That's part of the problem.

Think about it: How much time, energy, and money would *you* spend working on a personal problem you didn't realize you had? What if someone told you had a problem, but you just didn't believe it? How hard would you work to try to change it? Personality disorders are what is known as *low-insight conditions*, meaning that, by definition, the people who have these issues are not aware of them and will not acknowledge them when other people point them out.

So discuss these principles with a counselor, support group, or friends and family, and practice saying them to yourself:

High-conflict people have a narrow range of negative lifetime behavior that they repeat and repeat without changing, even when it is self-defeating.

Time and love will not change a high-conflict person for the better.

You cannot change a high-conflict person for the better.

Now that you know all of this, we hope you are starting to feel more confident in yourself. You can learn these dating radar skills and develop the ability to see into your own blind spots. It also really helps to have a good support system to help you stay balanced. After all, there are many good potential relationship partners out there; you just have to be able to screen out the high-conflict ones so you can find your way to the balanced, reasonable partners who can truly love you.

Jamming Your Radar

The next general skill is recognizing when someone is jamming your radar. High-conflict people do this using behaviors that can fool you or confuse you enough that you ignore all of their problematic patterns underneath the surface. Here are the four that our survey respondents noticed the most:

- Charm
- Fake compatibility
- Overt sexuality
- Protectiveness

Let's look briefly at each one.

Charm

As we mentioned throughout the book, charm was the most

noticeable behavior in dating partners who turned out to be high-conflict people. This doesn't mean that all charming people are high-conflict people. But it means that enough HCPs are extremely charming that you need to investigate and observe further. Don't just fall for their wiles and stop paying attention. Over time you will usually see whether the engaging wit, delightful sweetness, fascinating intelligence, or cheerful generosity falls away (as it did for many of our survey respondents), or if it lasts.

Entering a relationship should be no different than buying a car. Anyone can put a shiny coat of paint on it, add some nice wheels and new tires, but what really counts is what's under the hood. Is the transmission about to go out? Does the gas pedal have a tendency to stick? Do the brakes work? Take your time, do your research, and go for a good, long test drive.

As one of our respondents said, look for someone who is a 7 or 8, not someone who is a 10. This applies in terms of charm as well as many of the other characteristics. If the person seems too good to be true, they probably are. Just don't base your decisions about future commitments on the delights of the present. Look beyond the charm.

Fake Compatibility

Is your dating partner surprisingly compatible with your needs and interests? Are you amazed at how similar the two of you are? This compatibility might be genuine. But it might also be a fake. So this is another area in which to be watchful.

See if you can find out what the person's and passions or hobbies were a year ago; or several years ago. See how much they really know in this supposedly shared area of interest. Some people are like chameleons: they take up the pastimes or politics of whomever they are with. While this may be natural to some extent for young lovers who haven't developed all of their own tastes or beliefs yet, it may not be a good sign if they are trying to fake their interest. Sometimes you'll have to rely on your own gut feeling to tell truthfulness from fakery. But, if you can, talk to people who have known your dating partner for many years, and you will get a bigger picture that will tell you a lot.

Overt Sexuality

Overt sexuality was the third most common trait our survey respondents mentioned, and it's one of the most confusing ways of having your radar jammed. It's natural to be excited about a new partner and to want to be sexual with someone who you are attracted to. And especially if you're kind of shy or reserved, it can be very appealing to have someone come on strong.

The old taboos and rules against sex before marriage have pretty much fallen away in many cultures, including ours. But sexual attraction isn't very helpful in terms of choosing "the one." In fact, it will just cloud your judgment. Remember the brain chemicals that want you to fall deeply in love after having sex—dopamine, oxytocin, and endorphins—and how they alter your perception and memory.

Some of our respondents advised delaying sex as long as possible. It's unlikely that abstinence is going to be practiced in most dating relationships for very long. But it's very revealing to see what your partner's reaction is when you say you want to wait for a while.

If you decide to hop in the sack, be wise about it and realize it may alter your judgment. Our ancient brain chemistry wants us to fall in love and have babies as soon as possible. So you may have to override that chemistry when it comes to making decisions about a long-term commitment.

Here again, get help from friends if you want to screen out high-conflict people, who may be very fun, attractive, charming—*and* fabulous lovers. Ask your friends, "Am I missing something here? This person really seems great!"

Protectiveness

Both offers of protection and pleas for protection can also be very confusing. Many of us have been conditioned by our culture to want a Prince Charming or Sleeping Beauty. And, we are taught that if someone really needs us, we should step up. Yet, as we mentioned in chapter 9, one of the common blind spots is the idea that we're seeking our "better half." We look for someone who offers what we need—or needs what we offer. In this way, we kind of seduce ourselves.

Instead, we need to do what it takes to feel like a whole person on our own, so that we will be interdependent with a partner, not dependent on a partner. In reality, when a high-conflict person advertises how protective they will be, it's fake. Because they can't fulfill that for another adult. When someone insists that we take care of them, that's equally problematic, and for the same reason: it's too much to ask. We can help each other as whole people, but we can't fix another person or fill their unfillable holes. Promises of protectiveness generally are a mask for desires for dependency.

We hope that by sharing more about these radar-jamming characteristics of high-conflict people, we have prepared you to be more watchful and aware. So many of our survey respondents said that they wished they had known things like this before they made their commitments to partners who turned out to have high-conflict personalities.

Radar Up for High-Conflict Personalities

Now that you've taken some steps to open your eyes to your blind spots and, perhaps, become less vulnerable to them, and you're now aware of common ways your radar can get jammed, it's time to review the basic patterns of high-conflict personalities. In chapters 4 through 7, we addressed ten to twelve patterns for each of the four HCPs we most commonly see. Let's review the main themes.

All High-Conflict People:
Preoccupation with blaming others
All-or-nothing thinking
Unmanaged emotions
Extreme behavior

A drive to be special and superior (narcissistic HCPs): These personalities tend to be over the top in their desire to show off and brag about themselves. Underneath it all, there lies a powerful fear of being inferior or powerless. They can be extremely charming, but also very demeaning and insulting. They lack empathy. Don't buy it when they say that you are lucky to be with them and shouldn't challenge them. In the extreme, they have narcissistic personality disorder.

A roller coaster pattern (borderline HCPs): These personalities have extreme mood swings, sudden and intense anger, and a powerful fear of abandonment. They can be very loving and friendly, but then go into a rage. Then they switch back again. They lack emotional stability. Don't get stuck trying to match their anger or trying to calm them by agreeing with them on everything. In the extreme, they have borderline personality disorder.

A scheming, conning pattern (antisocial HCPs): These are your con artists who intentionally lie and manipulate you to get what they want. They can be extremely charming, and can also draw you in by falsely telling you about how they have been victims of other people's bad behavior. Don't get stuck trying to convince them they lied to you and should apologize. They may try to hurt you or get power and control over you, and they enjoy it. They lack remorse. In the extreme, they have antisocial (sociopathic) personality disorder.

A very dramatic pattern (histrionic HCPs): People with this personality have a strong drive to be the center of attention, can have very intense emotions, and often tell exaggerated or made-up stories. They can draw you in with their exciting energy, but also wear you down with their demand for attention to their dramas. Don't get stuck listening to them and just trying to be polite, and don't try to fix their problems. It doesn't really help them, and you will just be frustrated. Don't let them tell stories about you that aren't true to other people. Let the other people know you don't agree. In the extreme, they have histrionic personality disorder.

The patterns of all four of these high-conflict personalities become obvious over time. However, they can seem very charming, intelligent, reasonable, and loving at the beginning of a relationship. That's why you need dating radar!

Some people have traits of two or more of these personality patterns. You can read the different chapters for more specifics of how these patterns work. In this book we haven't tried to teach you how to manage an ongoing relationship with people with these patterns. We have other books for that (check out our websites: **www.HighConflictInstitute.com** and **www. UnhookedMedia.com,** and check the Resource page at the end of this book). Instead, our focus has been on showing you how to spot these folks so you can consciously decide whether to split up with them or try to make it work.

Take Your Time

From the start of this book, we have encouraged you to take your time in getting to know your dating partners. Many of the indications of a high-conflict personality don't become apparent until months into a relationship. While some of our survey respondents said that the warning signs took years to show up, we believe most of these signs can be seen within a year, if you know what to look for—and you do, now that you've read this book.

We recommend waiting at least a year before getting married or having children. These are major commitments, and it's best not to make them until you've allowed enough time for your partner to show their true colors. Remember that many of our survey respondents emphasized that these commitments were what triggered a total change in their partner's behavior. Try to find out the full range of your partner's personality *before* you make these commitments.

Deciding to have sex, get engaged, or move in together may be somewhat less of a commitment than getting married, but still, each of these things gets you deeper into the relationship and therefore will make it harder to get out. So it makes sense to think carefully about whether and when to do these things. In some cases, you may want to take these steps to see what your dating partner is really like when more responsibility and closeness are expected. Still, wait at least a year before getting married or having children. This also goes for combining finances—another major commitment.

We always recommend getting a second and third opinion about your dating partner. One way to do this is to socialize together with other friends. This way you can see how they interact with other people, and your friends can see how your dating partner is treating you. If your friends have feedback for you, listen to it! You don't always have to take their advice, but it's wise to pay attention to their input. They are not blinded by love the way you might be, and they may be able to see things that you don't.

Here's what one of our survey respondents said about timing:

We knew each other for twenty years (first as coworkers). I was instantly attracted, then he introduced me to his fiancée. They married, and five years later I was on her side when he decided all he wanted in life was to be free and single. He and I were attracted to each other, but never went out or fooled around. I thought, Seems a little unstable to date while working together. Always found him sexy. Then...boom one day. Was engaged three months later, married six months after that. Just left him after ten years.

This example tells us a lot. First of all, there's the issue of working with someone. She knew him for many years as a coworker. Yet working with someone doesn't tell you much at all about what they will be like in a close relationship. High-conflict people may be very normal in workplace relationships, which typically aren't that close. Where they have trouble is in intimate relationships.

Second, she knew him when he got married and when he got divorced five years later. Knowing that he wanted to be "free and single" in itself may have been a warning sign. If he had a high-conflict personality, he would have a narrow pattern of behavior, which means that this would come up again and again. If your partner has left someone else for you, he may later leave you for someone else.

Third, they got together very quickly. Engaged in three months and married in six. We wonder: If she had waited a year, would she have found out that he was a high-conflict person?

In the survey, she went on to list reasons she was attracted to him:

He was flexible, adapted to my schedule, wants, and needs easily.

He promised to take care of me and my children.

I always found him sexy.

Do you recognize these as three out of our top four radar-jamming issues? Was it fake compatibility when he seemed to be compatible by adapting to her schedule, and wants and needs? Was it the appearance of protectiveness that helped jam her radar? Was overt sexuality a distraction from seeing his high-conflict potential? If she had read this book, would she have recognized these warning signs in advance and steered clear of this relationship? She told us she would not have gotten into this relationship if she had known at the beginning what she knew at the end.

Once they were married, she said, he "changed overnight."

What did he do? Rage, blame, telling stories that didn't match reality. This sounds like our high-conflict personalities—particularly borderline and narcissistic. It certainly is a good example of how high-conflict people can look really good for several months and then change overnight.

Asked what advice she would give to others, she said:

Wait two years...they can't fake it more than two years.

This is a helpful example of how time and information can make all the difference. When we suggest that you wait *at least* a year, we think of this as a minimum. Two years is not a bad idea. However, if our survey respondent had known the information in this book, we think—based on our experience and that of more than 200 survey respondents—she might have realized within one year what she could really expect.

What a Healthy Relationship Feels Like

If you've read this entire book, you've read over 75,000 words about negative, ugly relationships. We would be remiss if we didn't talk about the other side of the coin, the positive side—what a good relationship feels and looks like. This is most important if you've been divorced from an HCP or only dated HCPs and don't really know what a good relationship is supposed to feel like, or how a non-HCP treats the person they love most (or, for that matter, anyone in their lives). But it's probably equally important if you've never been romantically involved with an HCP, because you don't know how bad it can be. So, here goes:

You know you're in a healthy romantic relationship when:

- You are never called names, demeaned, put down, or humiliated

- ° You don't walk on eggshells (have to watch everything, or most things, you say or do)
- Your opinion matters
- You don't have to hide friendships with other people
- Your relationship is absent of extreme highs and extreme lows (a little boring is good)
- Your partner isn't constantly job-hopping, or always in crisis financially
- Your partner is stable
- Your partner doesn't have to be the center of attention
- Your partner is open-minded and oriented toward problem-solving
- You don't feel like a lifeline or air supply for your partner
- You don't feel responsible for your partner's well-being

And, the single most important sign you're in a healthy relationship:

- You feel that you can be yourself.

Kelly and Josh Revisited

Here's a final exercise that we hope will convince you, if nothing else has in this book, or if you really aren't sure that HCPs are to be avoided. Below, we've copied and pasted the story of Josh and Kelly from chapter 1 (p. 15)—this time striking out the high-conflict personality parts and adding a few new words (in bold). Everything else is the same. What percentage of the story is struck out? That's the percentage of your romantic relationship with an HCP that will be bad for you. In Kelly and Josh's story, it's well more than half. Wouldn't you prefer a relationship that's better than half bad?

Kelly and Josh met in college and were ~~instantly~~ attracted to each other. He was on the football team and she was a student intern helping out at their practices. The relationship progressed ~~quickly~~ from a first date to being exclusive in ~~just two weeks~~ six months. They gradually started ~~doing everything together~~ spending more time together, with groups of friends and on dates with just the two of them ~~and even kept in touch during classes through texts and messaging.~~

~~It wasn't long before Josh became more controlling of some aspects of their relationship, although the control was subtle. He told her when she could and couldn't attend his football games and who she could and couldn't be friends with. In the beginning, he wanted to spend every second with her, but before long he spent less time with her and more time with other people. He went out with friends whenever he wanted but made her feel bad about spending time with her friends. She didn't say a word when he was dismissive or critical or her—often in front of their friends. She did his homework for him and picked him up from parties at all times of the night. She would do anything for him, even though he didn't do much for her.~~ Kelly just wanted to be in a relationship. In fact, she felt that she needed to have a partner. Josh did too, but in a different way. He liked showing her off to his friends. ~~Although Kelly didn't seem aware of it, she was willing to go along with whatever he wanted.~~

It wasn't perfect, but whose relationship is? Once in a while Josh would write sweet love letters to Kelly, ~~which kept her in the game. Within three months she was pregnant, and two months later, just days after their graduation from college, they got married.~~

The honeymoon was short—just Saturday night and Sunday. On Monday he went back to work and Kelly spent time with her family who were in town for the wedding. Heading back home *after a day of sightseeing with her family, her car broke down on the freeway and, unfortunately, her cell phone was almost dead. She had just enough battery left to call for a tow truck, but then she was stuck with no way to reach Josh. Three hours passed before she was able to reach him, using the tow truck driver's phone.*

Kelly explained her situation and apologized profusely. ~~Instead of the~~ *Josh was understanding and compassionate and hopped in his car to pick her up right away.* ~~compassion she expected for someone in her situation, especially from the man she'd married just forty-eight hours earlier, Josh's reaction was the complete opposite. He began yelling at her, calling her every foul name in the book and accusing her of cheating on him. "You are a f——ing c—— who spreads her legs for every c—— that walks by! You whore! Get your ass home! Now! I don't care what excuse you have or how you get here, you f——ing bitch!" It didn't end there; he kept raging for five long minutes while the tow truck driver sat there, trying to pretend he wasn't hearing the tirade.~~

Relieved and feeling helped and taken care of, Kelly breathed a sigh of relief while she waited for Josh to pick her up. ~~Shocked, embarrassed, and in tears, she handed the phone back to the driver and began the dreaded trip home. In those few minutes on the phone, Kelly's life took a new direction. After the high of the wedding a couple of days earlier, her life and dreams crashed. She became terrified and obedient, like a beaten dog.~~

~~Kelly never told anyone that she always felt like she was walking on eggshells, being careful of what she did and said. Or that she had to wait for permission to go places and talk to certain people. Or that Josh was nice to her in private and demeaning in public. Or that she could tell by the tone he used with her whether someone else was giving him attention—he was nice to her when they weren't, and~~

~~nasty when they were. Or that she now weighed just 95 pounds, although her normal weight was around 135 pounds.~~

~~Kelly and Josh stayed married for a few years and had children, but eventually the bubble burst and she began fighting back, which led to more violence. Divorce wasn't far behind. The ramifications of this seven-year relationship shaped Kelly's future. Her confidence was depleted and her ability to pick a "good" guy in her future relationships was compromised. Some childhood trauma she had never dealt with now had new trauma piled on top of it—all of it affecting her relationships, her self-esteem, and even her career.~~

Striking everything high-conflict from the story shortens it significantly. The stricken parts are ugly. They put a knot in your stomach. That's why we hope you'll do yourself the kindness of using dating radar in your love life. You don't want someone to write a story about you someday that contains any high-conflict drama. And you don't want to be a news story about violence, abuse, arrest, or murder.

You may want to try the same exercise with your own story, if you've been in a high-conflict relationship. Write down a scenario you were in with your HCP, then go back through it and strike out the ugly parts. See what's left. That's the kind of love you want in your life.

Conclusion

They say that hindsight is 20/20 vision. Well, we think dating radar is just as good, almost as good as x-ray vision. After all, we have developed it from the wisdom and experience of hundreds of other people. The most important thing to remember: Take it slow, and keep your eyes open! Watch out for extremes:

extremely good as well as extremely bad. Both are warning signs.

Learn about your own blind spots, maybe by enlisting the help of a trusted therapist. Remember the key characteristics of high-conflict personalities. Be prepared for the ways these folks can jam your radar. Enjoy the first months of your relationship, but don't let the excitement of new love drown out your intuition. Remember, choosing your life partner and who will be your children's other parent is about managing risk. Watch for the warning signs. When your gut tells you something might be off, pay attention to it!

While the belief that everyone deserves a second chance may pull strongly on you, it's different with HCPs. Second chances become third chances, and fourth…and forever. Remember that having a high-conflict personality is a lifelong pattern. These folks rarely change. Give yourself the gift of HCP awareness and the discipline to make the right decisions for yourself. Ultimately, it's up to you!

Most importantly, keep in mind that you are a whole person on your own, and you deserve to be treated with respect. Life can be fun and satisfying whether or not you have a partner.

Resources

Dating Radar

www.dating-radar.com

This is the authors' (Bill Eddy and Megan Hunter) website that supports this book, *Dating Radar*. You can find:

- Tests to find out if you are dating someone with a high-conflict personality
- Test to assess your vulnerability and risk for dating someone with a high-conflict personality
- Online courses
- Webinars
- Story wall (to share your stories)
- Surveys for you to take, and read survey results
- Ask the experts

The Black Sheep Project

https://www.blacksheepproject.org/

Help for anyone suffering with Borderline Personality Disorder, their families and loved ones, and professionals and community who support and treat them.

PDAN (Personality Disorder Awareness Network)

http://www.pdan.org/

Dedicated to increasing public awareness of personality disorders, alleviating the impact of personality disorders on families, and preventing the development of personality disorders in children.

Teen Dating Abuse

http://www.gopurple.org/

Provides young people with education, victim advocacy services, and peer-to-per activism to prevent teen dating abuse and build healthy relationships. They use a research-based, data-driven, and youth-centered 3-step model to uproot the causes of power-based personal violence (bullying, dating abuse, domestic violence, sexual assault/rape, stalking, gender-based violence).

National Sexual Assault Hotline

https://www.rainn.org/

1-800-656-HOPE (4673)

The National Domestic Violence Hotline

http://www.thehotline.org/

1-800-799-7233

BPD Central

www.bpdcentral.com

Help for people who have a family member with borderline personality disorder (BPD) and narcissistic personality disorder (NPD). Books, informative website, and 20,000 member online family support community, Welcome to Oz.

Hope for BPD

http://www.hopeforbpd.com/

Consultation, family support, and evidence-based treatment for Borderline Personality Disorder and self-harming behaviors.

Acknowledgements

Bill Eddy

I want to acknowledge Megan, for pushing this book forward in the face of many distractions. It has been a great collaboration and surprisingly easy. Your point of view has greatly expanded the messages in this book and your writing style has livened up my own writing. (I can no longer remember who wrote which sentences!)

I also want to thank Jess Beebe and Susan LaCroix for their wise editing, which not only helped us see what needed to be added and what needed to be taken out, but also how to best communicate our information to a wide age-range. Our team at High Conflict Institute has sharpened our thinking and simplified our methods, so that we can help people in any age group in recognizing and managing their relationships with high-conflict people, whether at home, at work or in the community. Lastly, I want to thank Scott Edelstein, my literary agent, for his ongoing advice in writing and publishing.

Megan Hunter

Thanks to the men and women who have shared their heart-wrenching broken love stories with us over the past decade. Without these deeply personal experiences, the book wouldn't have life.

I'll add my thanks along with Bill's to Jess Beebe for guiding us through every stage of the book writing process, including an introduction to the talented Susan LaCroix. Both of you, through your understanding of the subject and your expertise in editing, elevated our work.

Bill, thank you for the structure and knowledge you bring to every project. Your devotion to getting it right, avoiding bias, and helping people have been and always will be the example I follow.

Most of all, thanks to my wonderful husband, Paul, who proved that a broken picker is repairable. And to my perfectly amazing kids, Mychael and Alison, Bryant and Lacey, and sweet Liz. This book is meant for you and your generation to avoid the mistakes of previous generations, and to give your children a healthy example to follow.

Thanks to Nicholas Boria, a bright star ready to burst rays of light on the neuroscience universe. You were a big help in shaping my thoughts. And to my friends, Lisa Johnson Stone, Sue Taylor, Annette Burns, Karen Adam, and Lynne Kenney for your encouragement over the years and for sharing your insight and wisdom to help shape this book. I'm forever in awe of you and grateful for your friendship.

About the Authors

Bill Eddy is an award-winning author, lawyer, therapist, mediator and the President of the High Conflict Institute. He developed the "High Conflict Personality" theory (HCP theory) and is an international expert on managing high-conflict disputes.

As an attorney, Bill is a Certified Family Law Specialist in California and the Senior Family Mediator at the National Conflict Resolution Center in San Diego. Prior to becoming an attorney in 1992, he was a Licensed Clinical Social worker with twelve years' experience providing therapy to children, adults, couples and families in psychiatric hospitals and outpatient clinics. He has taught Negotiation and Mediation at the University of San Diego School of Law for six years and he is on the part-time faculty of the Straus Institute for Dispute Resolution at the Pepperdine University School of Law and the National Judicial College.

www.highconflictinstitute.com

Megan Hunter, MBA, is an author, speaker, and expert on high-conflict disputes and complicated relationships. She is CEO of Unhooked Media, a U.S.-based media company focused on relationship and conflict revolution through print, digital and the spoken word. She is publisher at High Conflict Institute Press and its imprint Unhooked Books, and co-founder of the High Conflict Institute. She is a frequent guest on Sirius XM Satellite's The Doctor Show (psychiatry).

Megan trains legal, mental health, business, leadership groups, universities and other professionals across Australia, the U.S., Canada, and South Africa. She has strong policy and judicial training experience during her tenure at the Arizona Supreme Court and as a member of the Arizona Board of Psychologist Examiners. She is Project Manager of "We Got This" at The Black Sheep Project, and serves on the Advisory Board of the Personality Disorder Awareness Network.

www.meganhunter.me

31901060925411

CPSIA information can be obtained
at www.ICGtesting.com
Printed in the USA
LVOW03s0352171017
552685LV00002B/2/P